COUNTRY PATTERNS

COUNTRY PATTERNS
1841·1883

A Sampler of American Country Home & Landscape Designs from Original 19th Century Sources

EDITED BY DONALD J. BERG

Revised Second Edition

A Sterling/Main Street Book
Sterling Publishing Co., Inc.   New York

Library of Congress Cataloging-in-Publication Data

Country patterns, 1841-1883.

   Originally published: Country patterns. Rockville
Centre, NY: Antiquity Reprints, c1982.
  Includes index.
   1. Country homes—United States—Designs and plans.
2. Cottages—United States—Designs and plans.
3. Gardens—United States. I. Berg, Donald J.
NA7561.C67   1986   728.3'7'0973   86-19969

Text design by Donald J. Berg

10 9 8 7 6 5 4 3 2 1

A Sterling/Main Street Book

Published in 1990 by Sterling Publishing Company, Inc.
387 Park Avenue South, New York, N.Y. 10016
Second Revised Edition © 1986 by Donald J. Berg
Distributed in Canada by Sterling Publishing
℅ Canadian Manda Group, P.O. Box 920, Station U
Toronto, Ontario, Canada M8Z 5P9
Distributed in Great Britain and Europe by Cassell PLC
Artillery House, Artillery Row, London SW1P 1RT, England
Distributed in Australia by Capricorn, Ltd.
P.O. Box 665, Lane Cove, NSW 2066
Manufactured in the United States of America
All rights reserved

ISBN 0-55562-008-6

CONTENTS

...

About This Book

In paging through this book you'll be taking a firsthand look at our past. All of the material is reproduced directly from the time-worn pages of home plan "pattern" books and magazines that were originally printed between 1841 and 1883. Like the three-story barn that appeared in the April, 1870 issue of THE AMERICAN AGRICULTURIST and inspired the one below, in Meriden, New Hampshire, the designs that you'll see and the advice that you'll read actually guided last century's homebuilders.

If you're restoring a 19th Century country home, planning an authentic landscape, or even designing a new home, I hope that you'll find a little bit of the inspiration that they did. — Donald J. Berg

Photo courtesy of Laura Lichiello

A Foreword by A. J. Downing

THE HORTICULTURIST, 1848

A VERY LITTLE OBSERVATION will convince any one that, in the United States, a new era, in *Domestic Architecture*, is already commenced. A few years ago, and all our houses, with rare exceptions, were built upon the most meagre plan. A shelter from the inclemencies of the weather; space enough in which to eat, drink and sleep; perhaps some excellence of mechanical workmanship in the details; these were the characteristic features of the great mass of our dwelling-houses—and especially country houses—a few years ago.

There are, perhaps, few persons who have examined fully the effects of a general diffusion of good taste, of well being, and a love of order and proportion, upon the community at large. There are, no doubt, some who look upon fine houses as fostering the pride of the few, and the envy and discontent of the many; and—in some transatlantic countries, where wealth and its avenues are closed to all but a few—not without reason. But, in this country, where integrity and industry are almost always rewarded by more than the means of subsistence, we have firm faith in the *moral* effects of the fine arts. We believe in the bettering influence of beautiful cottages and country houses—in the improvement of human nature necessarily resulting to all *classes*, from the possession of lovely gardens.

The first motive which leads men to build good houses is, no doubt, that of increasing largely their own comfort and happiness. But it is easy to see that, in this country, where so many are able to achieve a home for themselves, he who gives to the public a more beautiful and tasteful model of a habitation than his neighbors, is a benefactor to the cause of morality, good order, and the improvement of society where he lives. To place before men reasonable objects of ambition, and to dignify and exalt their aims, cannot but be laudable in the sight of all. And in a country where it is confessedly neither for the benefit of the community at large, nor that of the succeeding generation, to amass and transmit great fortunes, we would encourage a taste for beautiful and appropriate architecture, as a means of promoting public virtue and the general good.

We have said beautiful and *appropriate* architecture—not without desiring that all our readers should feel the value of this latter qualification as fully as we do. Among the many strivings after architectural beauty, which we see daily made by our countrymen, there are, of course, some failures, and only now and then examples of perfect success. But the rock on which all novices split—and especially all men who have thought little of the subject, and who are satisfied with a feeble imitation of some great example from other countries—this dangerous rock is *want of fitness*, or *propriety*. Almost the first principle, certainly the grand principle, which an apostle of architectural progress ought to preach in America, is, "keep in mind PROPRIETY." Do not build your dwelling-houses like temples, churches, or cathedrals. Let them be, characteristically, dwelling-houses. And more than this; always let their individuality of purpose be fairly avowed; let the cottage be a cottage—the farm-house a farm-house—the villa a villa, and the mansion a mansion. Do not attempt to build a dwelling upon your farm after the fashion of the town-house of your friend, the city merchant; do not attempt to give the modest little cottage the ambitious air of the ornate villa. Be assured that there is, if you will search for it, a peculiar beauty that belongs to each of these classes of dwellings that heightens and adorns it almost magically; while, if it borrows the ornaments of the other, it is only debased and falsified in character and expression. The most expensive and elaborate structure, overlaid with costly ornaments, will fail to give a ray of pleasure to the mind of real taste, if it is not appropriate to the purpose in view, or the means or position of its occupant; while the simple farm-house, rustically and tastefully adorned, and ministering beauty to hearts that answer to the spirit of the beautiful, will weave a spell in the memory not easily forgotten.

THE neglected home, where the child grows up without knowledge of order or correct system; tools and vehicles exposed to all kinds of weather, rusting and falling to pieces from inattention.

THE home of neighbor Thrifty, where the children learn habits of neatness, economy and good management; there being a place for every implement when not in use, and each kept where it belongs.

HOUSES & COTTAGES

...

J.J. Thomas, THE REGISTER OF RURAL AFFAIRS, 1865

HOUSE is always a teacher; it may become an agent of civilization. While builders minister to deceit and vanity, those vices will prevail; when their works embody fitness, truth and dignified simplicity, these republican virtues will be firmly rooted in the nation. Few are aware how strong an influence is exerted by the dwelling on its inhabitants.

Mistakes in building are more often made through want of thought than lack of taste or means; still the consequences are equally serious.

To harmonize with the surrounding scenery, to enter into the spirit of the landscape, is the highest beauty of a domestic building. This is too often overlooked;—and we find the dignity and repose of Nature broken by the presence of white, bare, bleak abodes, set ostentatiously in unplanted fields. Flat roofs and horizontal lines are opposed to the ascending lines of rocks and mountains around them; lofty turrets and steep gables rise up to contradict the natural expression of level plains. A house may be considered beautiful in the situation which suits it; its precise copy, in an unfit place, will always be a miserable deformity.

Fashion is not the synonym of taste; nor is beauty monopolized by wealth. A low log-cabin, nestled in the woods, the moss grown over its roof, the morning-glories climbing to the rustic window, is more attractive and is a better home than many a costly marble mansion. But the effort of "putting the best foot foremost," and anxiously attempting much display, costs our country homes the truth, the comfort, the sobriety which ought to characterize their architecture.

No house can fail to please whose form and hue accord with the adjacent country; which looks just what it is, neither less nor more; whose proportions and details are formed upon the principles of taste; and whose inner arrangement regards economy of space and gives attention to the laws of health,—requiring the fewest steps, presenting the greatest cheerfulness, neatness and convenience for common and daily use. All which the poorest man who builds can have as well as the rich; for Providence opens a short road to comfort, but hedges up the path to luxury.

A SMALL COTTAGE.

This design, being intended for a respectable family of limited means, who desire a home of their own, however humble, has been supplied, to meet the wants of such, with every facility for refined domestic life; although, of course, in a small way.

There is but one large room for general family use, but this is furnished with a pantry 5 by 8 feet, and a platform adjoining the wood-house, where, in mild weather, much coarse work may be performed. From this the cellar stairs descend, directly under the flight to the upper story. The closet in

Fig. 3.—*First Floor.*

this platform may be constructed only three feet high, to contain iron ware, and the top of it can be used as a table for washing dishes. The sliding window in the pantry will allow the replacing of the dishes without taking them around through the living-room door. The platform being in the body of the house, is simply enclosed on its outer side by the studding of the walls—in this a door-way should be made to allow free access to the wood-house.

There is a large bed-room on the first floor, having two closets. (The place most suitable for the bed is marked by a parallelogram crossed by diagonal lines; and all the doors in this and the succeeding plans are marked with dotted lines, showing in what direction they should swing back.) The upper story is occupied by two bed-rooms and a bath-room. The garrets are obtained by enclosing the sloping space on each side of the chambers, thus leaving them of proper height throughout.

Fig. 4.—*Chamber Floor.*

The right hand chimney, rising only from the second floor, should be solidly supported by thick planks in that part of the floor where it stands, to prevent its settling. The stove-pipe from the living-room fire passes up into the room above to enter the chimney.

The body of the house is 25 by 34 feet, with a wing 12 by 17 feet.

Cost of Erection.—The cost of building in accordance with these designs will vary much with the degree of finish and price of materials, and the estimates furnished can be considered only as approximate ones. They are made, in all instances, on the basis of prices before the war, to which the requisite additions must be made in accordance with the increased rates. The estimates are also intended for wood—if built of stone or brick, nearly one-half more should be added, varying with localities.

The cost of a house built according to the preceding design, would be from twelve to fifteen hundred dollars.

A BRACKETED SQUARE HOUSE.

The building, plainly and neatly constructed of wood, **and vertically boarded**, would cost, before the war, eighteen hundred **to two thousand dollars**. It is thirty-three feet square and one story and **a half in height;** the lower story should be nine feet high, and the upper one five feet **on the sides**, when finished, **and as much higher in the centre as desired.**

On the first floor there is a parlor, bed-room, sitting-room and **kitchen—** the last two communicating by an entry from which the cellar stairs de-

Fig. 6.—*First Floor.*   Fig. 7.—*Chamber Floor.*

scend. Both bed-room and kitchen open into an entry with an **outside door,** whose left-hand side is occupied with shelves for kitchen use, or a sink or the water-pump might be placed there, as the convenience of the family might most require.

The stairs which lead to the chambers are near the bed-room door—an advantage to the mistress of the house in case of sickness. The two right-hand rooms on the second floor are adapted to family use, one of them having a door into the bath-room, and both being connected by a lighted passage, with shelves on one side, as in the one below. All the bed-rooms are furnished with closets, and are nearly equal in size.

A PLAIN COUNTRY HOUSE.

This dwelling, neat and cheerful in its exterior, is 32 by 35 feet in size, and so simple in the arrangement of its rooms as to require little explanation.

The parlor and sitting room are entered by a small passage-way opening on the veranda in front. A side hall connects with the three principal rooms, and contains the stair-case. The kitchen is entered through the sitting-room, and has a pantry adjoining.

The upper rooms are equal in size to those below them, and are furnished with closets; between two of them a small bathing-room is situated. The recess, 5 by 8 feet, in the right-hand front bed-room, forms a pleasant place for sewing or study; or may be set off by a partition to form a separate room.

Fig. 10.—*Chamber Floor.*

Fig. 9.—*First Floor.*

The expense would be about the same as in the preceding design.

A CONVENIENT DWELLING.

The plan affords a parlor, sitting-room, kitchen and seven bed-rooms, and is adapted to the use of a large family residing in a country village or on a farm of moderate size.

The front porch may be fitted with glazed windows and a door in winter, in order to add to the warmth of the hall. The sitting or dining-

Fig. 12.—*First Floor.*

Fig. 13.—*Chamber Floor*

room is separated from the kitchen by the pantry—an arrangement which is approved by all who have tried it; as it excludes much noise and smoke from the dining-room, while the pantry is accessible to both rooms at once.

The wing is not as high as the main part of the house in either story—the difference between the height of the lower rooms requiring that the bed-rooms in the upper story of the wing should be entered from the landing of the stairs; a few more steps lead to the upper hall and the front rooms.

There are several points in which this design may be modified to suit different tastes and requirements. Most persons would prefer a sliding window, or no connection at all, between the bed-room on the first floor and the kitchen. Some might wish a door in the parlor to open on the little back porch, instead of a window opening from the floor by weights and pulleys; or choose to employ the airy and pleasant little bed-room, 8 by 11, above stairs, as a study or sewing room. These changes are easily made.

The cost of this building would be about two thousand two hundred dollars.

[The engraving of the perspective view is defective in some particulars, but serves to give the general expression.]

A LARGE FARM-HOUSE.

In the erection of this class of dwellings, we need to strike a happy medium between the unsuitable and profuse adornment sometimes used, and

Fig. 15.—*First Floor.*

total disregard of taste and the neglect of every mental and social requirement. More of the real character of the country gentleman should be expressed—his culture without foppishness—honesty without rudeness.

Upon this principle the present design is believed to be based. While every facility for household labors is presented, there is scope offered for home comfort, intellectual improvement and wide hospitality.

The front rooms are so placed, that they must be more or less used by the family. The house consists of two buildings, a large one in front and a small one in the rear,—connected by the kitchen, which is only one story in height, with a lofty ceiling following up the slope of the rafters, so as to be high in the centre; lighted by windows on each side, and surrounded by all the closets, &c., required in domestic labor. The wood closet must be kept filled with wood, cut ready for use in a detached wood-house. The dairy or milk-room has an outer door of its own, and a large closet for keeping cheese. This closet is so situated that the odor of the cheese is not likely to fill the house. The cellar stairs are easily accessible from kitchen, dairy and back kitchen, and the stairs to the back chambers can be used by the hired men without their entering the other rooms, as the passage leading to them opens out-of-doors. The large and pleasant sitting-room is near

Fig. 16.—*Chamber Floor.*

the kitchen, the front stair-case and two bed-rooms. Some of the doors to the upper rooms should be partially glazed, to admit enough light to the upper hall; or the small bed-room might be omitted and the hall thus lighted by the front window. The four other bed-rooms are all large, of equal size, and furnished with ample closet-room. The upper room on the right hand, (being reached only by an entry,) is more retired than the rest, and would be comfortable and quiet for an invalid.

The upper floor of the rear building is occupied by two good bed-rooms, for the use of domestics, &c., closets being made next to the eaves. A gable-window lights the space between the rooms. Cost, about $3,300.

THIS design was drawn by us for the Rev. John D. McClintock, Huntingdon, West Va. It is one of those American cottages containing very liberal accommodations for a small family. Its cost, finely finished, of bricks, painted neat, with porches and well-finished interior, was $3446.25; built of frame, would cost $3000. It is slated with slates from the True Blue Quarry, Pennsylvania. These slates come very regular in color, are durable and strong; ornamentally laid, they cost 12 cents per square foot. The hall and parlor are finished in chestnut and other natural woods, oiled and rubbed down. Care has been taken with the proportions. The windows are large, and the interior is finished with heaters, slate mantels, and range complete for this sum. Such buildings are needed, and we design numbers of them for various persons all over the country. They sell at good price and give universal satisfaction. Every situation demands different treatment, and the arrangements of the rooms can be suited to any locality and the taste of the owner.

First Floor.—P, parlor, 15 by 16 feet; F R, family-room, 15 by 16 feet; O, office, 15 by 16 feet; D R, dining-room, 12 by 14 feet; K, kitchen, 10 by 11 feet; B R, bath-room, 6 by 7 feet; P, pantry; H, hall, 6 feet.

Second Floor.—C, chamber, 15 by 16 feet; C, chamber, 15 by 16 feet.

An American Cottage

Isaac H. Hobbs, HOBBS' ARCHITECTURE, 1876

FIRST FLOOR.

SECOND FLOOR.

Cottage

H.W. Cleveland, William & Samuel D. Backus, VILLAGE AND FARM COTTAGES, 1856

Kitchen and
Living Room
14 × 14

Pantry

Parlor

12 × 12

FIRST FLOOR PLAN

Bed
8.9 × 9.4

Bed
8.9 × 14

c / c

12 × 15
Bedroom

SECOND FLOOR PLAN

PERSPECTIVE VIEW.

A Village House

Calvert Vaux & F.S. Withers, VILLAS & COTTAGES, 1864

PLAN OF PRINCIPAL FLOOR.

PLAN OF CHAMBERS.

THIS house was built for Dr. J. K. Lee, Chestnut Street, West Philadelphia, and is very generally admired. The house is built of brown stone, with roof of tin, and is not less attractive than comfortable.

The accommodations provided for, by the plan of the principal floor, consist of a fine projecting veranda porch, which gives access to the hall, office, drawing-room, dining-room, and stair-hall. The dining-room and parlor have each a bay-window, decorated with stained glass. The accommodations for the culinary department are ample, there being both a kitchen and an out-kitchen. There is also a spacious pantry upon this floor.

This house was built in 1866, and cost, when completed, between $6000 and $8000.

First Floor—1, reception-hall, 8 by 10 feet; 2, office, 10 by 12 feet; 3, stair-hall, 7 feet; 4, parlor, 16 by 22 feet; 5, dining-room, 15 by 20 feet 6 inches; 6, kitchen, 16 by 16 feet 6 inches; 7, pantry, 7 feet 6 inches by 4 feet 6 inches; 8, out-kitchen, 9 feet 6 inches by 7 feet 6 inches; 9, 10, porch.

Second Floor.—11, dressing-room, 10 by 9 feet 6 inches; 12, bath-room, 10 by 11 feet; 13, entry; 14, closet; 16, chamber, 16 by 22 feet; 17, chamber, 10 by 13 feet; 18, hall; 19, chamber, 10 by 14 feet; 20, closet; 21, nursery, 16 feet 6 inches by 16 feet; 22, 23, veranda.

A House in the Italian Style

Isaac H. Hobbs, HOBBS'S ARCHITECTURE, 1876

FIRST FLOOR.

SECOND FLOOR.

A Picturesque Stone Cottage

BEAUTY of outline and proportion is as important in the design and construction of a house, as the interior arrangement of the dwelling. A "square box' may afford all necessary facilities to the family, but if it does not please the eye and gratify the esthetic as well as the animal wants, it lacks an indispensable part of what a fine country house ought to be. The large number of houses which have been put up during the last three or four years on the great thoroughfares of travel leading out of New York, have afforded a good opportunity for the exercise of the talents of our Architects, and the skill of our suburban Builders. The design we give (No. 1) was executed of stone, at " Highwood Park," Tenafly Station, on the line of the Northern New Jersey Rail Road, and situate on the western Palisade slope.

Fig. 1, is a perspective view, and Figs. 2 and 3 are first and second floor plans. The style is a modification of the Gothic, with "bell-cast" roof. The main building is 17 x 30 feet, and the extension 20 x 21 feet. The whole, two stories and attic, with a cellar and a basement kitchen below. Exposure, south-westerly. The first floor, Fig. 2, contains: L, lobby, 5 x 8 feet; P, parlor, 13½ x 14 feet; D, dining-room, 14 x 17½ feet; H, open hall and stair-case; K, kitchen, 13 x 14 feet, besides sink-room, pantry and china-closet. Fig. 3, is the second floor plan, containing three sleeping rooms, 13 x 14 feet; a bath-room, 6 x 10 feet, with a passage for communication from front to rear rooms, and wardrobe at the side; c, c, are closets. The attic contains space for four rooms, about 8 x 10 and 12 feet. The parlor and dining room are separated by folding doors, and may be *en suite* when required; and are warmed, with the chambers above them, by the furnace.

Cost.—The cost of the house, including a well, entrance gates, grading and walks, will not exceed $6,000. The following are the principal items of cost. The walls, the most costly item, were laid up in random courses of silicious, or sand stone, white and red, and contain about—

5,000 cubic feet of stone work at 30c.,	$1,500 00
(This includes pointing and excavation for cellar.)	
8,000 feet timber and rough lumber at 24-00,	192 00
Shingles, lath, flooring, finishing pine, architraves and moulds, &c., cartage and freight,	850 00
Sashes, doors and blinds,	368 00
Lathing and plastering, cistern and chimneys,	375 00
Carpenter work, about 275 days, at $3,	825 00
Painting,	250 00
Plumbing, (pump, sink and piping),	80 00
Furnace and setting,	250 00
Hardware, about,	200 00
Lightning conductors,	68 00
Speaking tubes,	15 00
The wells walks, grading and gates,	700 00

Daniel T. Atwood, COUNTRY & SUBURBAN HOUSES, 1871

Samuel Sloan, HOMESTEAD ARCHITECTURE, 1861

An Irregular Bracketed Country House

WE might, with almost equal propriety, have termed this a farm-house. The only objection to this is the probability of impressing the reader with the idea that its application would be accordingly restricted. Indeed, it almost deserves the name of VILLA; but the total absence of ostentation in its external aspect inclines us to the appellation we have bestowed upon it, notwithstanding the villa-like extent of its accommodations. Plain, sensible, and solid, it is within the reach and applicable to the circumstances of many who love convenience without ambitious display, and who prefer dignified plainness to gingerbread ostentation. Architecturally, this design aims at being a country dwelling, manifesting the dignity, comfort, and substantial character of social life that is attainable in the country. There is a growing demand for this class of dwellings. Farmers are becoming rich, merchants and manufacturers are retiring from business; and we know that while the frank modesty of the farmer seldom allows him to aspire to towers or pinnacles, nine out of ten of retired citizens are too plain and practical in their views to seek for more than the embodiment of the various accommodations suited to their modes of life, at the lowest grade of expense requisite to give them a tasteful and substantial home. Since we have held these points in view, our motive for the comprehensive appellation "country-house" will be at once perceived. Suggestive not only of home comfort, but of the pleasure of social existence, the internal arrangements are in conformity to the demands of a life of business or a life of leisure, while the outward evidence, furnished by the elevation, goes far to sustain the idea that the proprietor, if not in possession of an unlimited store of wealth, has been touched by the spirit of elevated taste, and has declared his inspiration in language susceptible of no double meaning.

ACCOMMODATION.—A veranda G, fig. 1, furnishes the entrance way to the main hall D. A drawing-room A, 14 by 26 feet, entered by folding doors from the hall, forms a very interesting portion of this plan, on account of relative situation, its modest little bay-window, and the adjoining veranda, which is approached through lengthened windows, and communicates in the same manner with the sitting-room. This sitting-room, marked B, is 22 by 14 feet, and communicates directly with the drawing-room and main hall. This hall is 12 feet square, and a passage, containing the main stairway, leads to the rear entrance, and affords communication with the kitchen and private stairs. An arch thrown over the stair passage, at its junction with the hall D, will give the latter a complete individuality, and will be not only productive of effect as a feature, but gives opportunity for the introduction of a separate and dissimilar cornice, and, in short, establishes for the main hall a character exclusively its own.

A dining-room, 17 by 24 feet, furnished with china closet, and entered from the main hall, is located in the front portion of the house. With the facilities attendant on the mode of service which generally obtains in the style of living of which this house is assumed to be an exponent, all the fixtures of the table can be promptly removed, and the apartment, under the auspices of youthful management, becomes a scene of social and even sportive enjoyment. The private stairs are situated between the dining-room and kitchen, communicating with a small lobby, which is intended for a passage between these apartments. The kitchen E, 14 by 20 feet, is pro-vided with a side entrance, and a very respectable appendage, 12 by 14 feet, which may be used as a pump-shed, wood house, or bakery. In the latter case a suitable oven will be built, so as to vent its smoke into the kitchen chimney.

By reference to the plan of the second floor, fig. 2, it will be observed that the chambers are respectively designated by the letter H. I is the hall, and K the roofs of verandas. Good bed-rooms may be fitted up in the *garret*, care being taken to provide for their ventilation, in addition to that afforded by the gable windows.

CONSTRUCTION.—Brick, rough cast, with wooden cornices, and slate or shingle roof, may be indicated as the essential components of this structure. The verandas, however, require metallic roofing. The window-heads and sills should be stone. There is no absolute objection to building the walls of rubble-stone. The effect of this would be to make it look more essentially the home of the farmer "to the manor born."

ESTIMATE.—Built in the manner above described, the cost of this dwelling would not vary much from $7500.

THIS design is a beautiful type of an American home. We have many orders for drawings of such styles of houses. Some people persist in filling their houses with closets, and, when in excess, they become hiding-places. There should be a commodious closet and clothes-press in every chamber. The kitchen should have ample places for its necessary articles; the store-room, butler's pantry, are all needed. This building can be built for $2500 very complete, by good superintendence on the part of the owner in purchasing materials, and seeing that they are used economically. The house is of frame, covered with felt and weather-boarding; this felt is now manufactured quite thick, and nailed upon the studding. The roof may be shingles or slate; there is an air-space or loft above the second floor. An open communication from below the cornice must be made to communicate with it all around, and there must be two flues, one open at the bottom of this loft, and passing through the roof, and the other open at the top of loft, and opening out high above. This insures a constant change of air in the vault, and renders the upper rooms cool and comfortable at all times.

First Floor.—H, hall, 10 feet wide; P, parlor, 16 by 22 feet; S R, sitting-room, 16 by 18 feet; D R, dining-room, 14 by 22 feet; C, chamber, 14 by 18 feet; K, kitchen, 14 by 18 feet.

Second Floor.—C, chamber, 16 by 22 feet; C, chamber, 10 by 10 feet; C, chamber, 16 by 18 feet; C, chamber, 14 by 18 feet; C, chamber, 14 by 22 feet; C, chamber, 14 by 18 feet.

An American Cottage

Isaac H. Hobbs, HOBBS'S ARCHITECTURE, 1876

FIRST FLOOR.

SECOND FLOOR.

Cottage

WE show here a compact, convenient cottage, having a conservatory attached for those who love to gratify their taste for flowers. Each room has a cross draft, and can be abundantly ventilated in warm weather. A passage between the kitchen and dining-room cuts off the smell of cooking, and the doors from the kitchen are double, with spring-hinges, and without locks or other fastenings; they are opened with the foot, and close immediately after passing. The servant can pass in the kitchen through one door and out through the other with a large tray of dishes, and thus avoid meeting any one, while flies and the aroma of cooking have little chance of getting into the main part of the house. We think during the summer months it adds much to the comfort of all country houses to put in the windows the neat, modern wire-gauze window-guard, which does not obstruct air or sight, and does keep out effectually flies, millers, gnats, beetles, spiders, mosquitoes, bats, cats, and the whole list of nuisances against which we make our rooms close and dismal, and mope in summer evening darkness to avoid. The safety, cleanliness, and comfort of an open country house, night and day, can thus be enjoyed; light, sunshine, and fresh air can be had in abundance, and a feeling of comfort insured which those who have once tried it would never be without.

FIG. 1.—CELLAR PLAN.

FIG. 2.—FIRST FLOOR.

FIG. 3.—SECOND FLOOR.

George E. & F.W. Woodward, ARCHITECTURE, LANDSCAPE GARDENING AND RURAL ART, 1867

FIG. 1.—CELLAR PLAN.

FIG. 2.—FIRST FLOOR.

FIG. 3.—SECOND FLOOR.

Cottage

THIS design can, for the amount of room afforded, be constructed very cheaply. The kitchen is shown in the basement plan, but can be put on the first floor, or in a rear addition, if deemed more convenient. If built in an exposed situation, some filling-in between the studding will be necessary. There are several modes of doing this, all of which add to the stiffness and solidity of the frame, and ward off the searching winds. An air chamber for confined or dead air adds much to winter warmth and summer coolness, and this is usually provided for. The most common mode of filling-in is with soft brick laid on edge in mortar; grout is also made use of. Back plastering, or lathing between studs—nailing common laths or rough pieces against strips fastened to each side of the studs and covered with coarse mortar—is serviceable. Where lumber is plenty, cover the frame with rough boards, and put the weather-boarding on the outside of the rough boarding; this we have found answers an excellent purpose. A layer of common tarred roofing-paper between the two courses of boarding will render the house impenetrable to wind or rain, and affords one of the best means of protection.

A Small Rural Double Cottage

A SMALL RURAL DOUBLE COTTAGE. - for two small families. Under the farmer's living-room is a basement-kitchen, with the windows considerably out of ground, and under the coachman's kitchen is a cellar: the entrances are, as will be perceived, quite distinct. Up stairs the farmer has three bedrooms; the coachman but one, according to instructions. Such a cottage would cost about $1800, neatly finished.

Such a plan would not be unsuitable for a lodge, in which the families of a gardener and gate-keeper could live, or it might be fitted up a little more completely, and offer convenient accommodation to two friends who felt inclined to build it on some agreeable rural lot for a few months' quiet residence in the summer.

It seems strange that this idea should not be more frequently acted on than is the case at present. Far away from the fashionable watering-places, but easily accessible from the cities—in the heart of Vermont, for instance—may be found bold, beautiful scenery, pure air, and a pleasant neighborhood. Land is cheap, timber cheap, living cheap, and all of the best. These are the spots that should attract the attention of heads of families who wish to give their young people the benefit of country life in the summer.

PLAN OF PRINCIPAL FLOOR.

Calvert Vaux, VILLAS AND COTTAGES, 1857

THIS design is one of those that meet with more admirers in this country than any other class of buildings. We send throughout the North, South, East and West, perhaps twenty similar designed buildings in a year, of this type, varied in their evolutions to suit different grounds and surroundings; also different plans, the number of rooms, closets, etc., are made to suit circumstances; also changes for different kinds of materials to be used in the construction, some of wood, as the above, others pointed stone, others brick, painted. The beauty rests in the proportions and treatment. The house can be built, completely finished, with all the modern improvements, hot and cold water, heater, and gas pipes throughout, for from $4000 to $7000, according to the expensive character of the materials used.

First Floor.—A, parlor, 12 by 18 feet; B, porch; D, office, 15 by 15 feet; R, kitchen, 12 by 13 feet 6 inches; F, dining-room, 15 by 12 feet.

Second Floor.—C, principal chamber, 12 by 18 feet; H, chamber, 15 by 12 feet; P, chamber, 10 by 12 feet; N, chamber, 15 by 15 feet.

A Village House

Isaac H. Hobbs, HOBBS'S ARCHITECTURE, 1876

FIRST FLOOR.

SECOND FLOOR.

Cottage

A.J. BICKNELL, BICKNELL'S VILLAGE BUILDER, 1872

FIRST FLOOR PLAN.

A Semi-Southern Cottage

This is a house well adapted to the Middle and Southern States, although for the latter a veranda should be thrown around the front and sides.

FIRST FLOOR PLAN.

SECOND FLOOR PLAN.

A—Reception Room..... 9.0 × 11.6
B—Conservatory .... 9.0 × 11.6
C—Dining Room.. ..18.0 × 25.0
D—Parlor..........18.0 × 25.0
E—Hall .... 8.6 wide
F—Pantry............ 5.0 × 9.0
G—Kitchen..... ...13.6 × 18.0
H—Breakfast Room.....11.0 × 13.6
X—Store Room........ 4.6 × 9.6
K—Closets. .... 4.6 wide
L—Back Hall ....

A—Dressing Room..... 9.0 × 11.0
B—Boudoir............ 8.6 × 9.0
C—Dressing Room..... 9.0 × 11.6
D—Bed Room.........11.0 × 18.0
E—Hall.............. 8.6 wide
F—Bed Room........18.0 × 25.0
G—Balcony ....
H—Bed Room........11.0 × 18.0
I—Closets............ ....
J—Cedar Closet.......
K—Bed Room........13.6 × 15.0
L—Bath..............
M—Bed Room........11.6 × 13.6
N—Back Hall......... 4.6 wide
O—Lumber Room..... 4.6 × 9.6

D.H. Jacques, THE HOUSE, 1859

THIS cottage was designed for a gentleman in Salem, Ill. The superstructure is of brick, and the roof of slate, cut in ornamental shapes. It contains ample accommodations for a small family, and possesses conveniences, such as bath-room, water-closet, low-down grates, etc. The exterior is very pleasing, and is capable of a much higher degree of ornamentation than is shown in the engraving. The house can be built for $5000. It can be modified to preserve the external appearance; yet, by leaving out such conveniences as bath-room, etc., which can be added to the house at any time in the future, it can be built for $3000, if built of frame.

First Floor.—A, hall; B, sitting-room, 16 by 16 feet; C, parlor, 16 by 20 feet; D, dining-room, 13 feet 11 inches by 20 feet; E, kitchen, 13 feet 11 inches by 12 feet; F, scullery, 8 feet 5 inches by 6 feet 4 inches; G, china-closet; H, sewing-room, 10 by 6 feet 4 inches.

Second Floor.—I, bath-room, 5 feet 2 inches by 8 feet; J, bed-room, 8 feet 6 inches by 10 feet; K, chamber, 13 feet 4 inches by 15 feet 2 inches; L, chamber, 13 feet 4 inches by 12 feet; M, chamber, 13 feet 8 inches by 15 feet 11 inches; N, chamber, 18 feet 9 inches by 15 feet; O, hall; P, balcony.

A Cottage in the Pointed Style

Isaac H. Hobbs, HOBBS'S ARCHITECTURE, 1876

FIRST FLOOR.

SECOND FLOOR.

The accompanying plan of a rural cottage was awarded a premium which was offered some few years ago. The outside appearance is attractive, light and pleasant, and is not over-ornamental, a great fault with many modern houses. The rooms are large and most conveniently arranged, every room of the ground floor being pleasant enough for a parlor or a living-room.

PEALE'S POPULAR EDUCATOR, 1883

A Rural Cottage

inches by 14 feet 6 in. ; *Library*, 15 feet by 14 feet 6 inches; *Kitchen*, 12 feet 6 inches by 13 feet 6 inches; *Wash-Room*, 12 feet by 8 feet; *Hall*, 6 feet 5 inches in width.

SECOND STORY.

A, bed-room, 14 feet 5 inches by 11 feet 9 inches; *B*, chamber, 18 feet 9 inches by 15 feet; *C, C,* halls; *D*, bed-room, 9 feet 6 inches by 11 feet; *E*, bed-room, 14 feet 6 inches

GROUND PLAN.

D. R., dining-room, 18 feet 9 inches by 15 feet; *Parlor*, 18 feet 9 by 11 feet; *F*, servants' bed-room, 12 feet 6 inches by 14 feet 6 inches; *G*, passage, 3 feet 6 inches in width.

GROUND PLAN.

SECOND STORY.

A Bracketed American Cottage

1

WE mean what we say when we pay this design the high compliment of calling it American, and we think our readers will sustain us in the application of the very comprehensive term. Simple in form, convenient and economical in arrangement, tasteful yet unassuming in detail, we know of no title so expressive of its deserts as the one we have given it. Although it possesses no trait preventive of its recognition as an important country residence in any part of the Union, we conceive that it would be a decidedly acceptable dwelling to the well-to-do resident of the Western prairie. The umbrage afforded the windows by the canopies and balconies, while enhancing the boldness of the design, contributes greatly to the comfort of the apartments by protecting the glass from the noonday summer sun, even in the Northern and Western States.

CONSTRUCTION.—The great abundance of wood in some portions of our country, the facility with which it is transported from a timber region to a prairie, and the ease with which it is adapted to building, will be reason enough for using it for that purpose for generations to come. The design before us is intended to be constructed of wood.

ESTIMATE.—An excellent and substantial house may be built after this plan for $3700, in any part of Pennsylvania,—the stories being 10 and 9 feet in the clear respectively; the exterior painted a warm, drab color, slightly tinged with blue, and the roof covered with white pine shingles, about 5 inches or one-third their length to the weather.

ACCOMMODATION.—From the front piazza F, fig. **1.** the passage of 6 feet wide is entered, which gives access to all the rooms; an outside entrance is also given in the end of the building through the stair hall. A, 16 by 20 feet, is designed for a parlor; B, 16 by 16 feet, is a sitting-room; C, 16 by 20 feet, a dining-room; D, 16 by 16 feet, a kitchen; and E, a pantry, affording also a passage from dining-room to kitchen. We may remark here, that a veranda extending the full length of parlor and dining-room would be a very beneficial addition to this design, both for use and appearance. In accordance with the apparent demand for such an improvement, we have shown it in the perspective.

Cottage in the Rural Gothic Style

WHILE we have endeavored to concentrate within moderate limits the necessary conveniences of a comfortable mode of living for the occupants, we have not neglected the outward expression of taste that contributes so largely to the pleasure of the beholder. A plain building, by a few, simple, well-directed touches, can thus be invested with a character approaching the ornate. A brief analysis of the design before us will attest the truth of the above remark. Remove first the barge and eave treatment, and we destroy at once the *polish* of the expression; but take away the pinnacles, and we greatly weaken the expression itself, almost entirely depriving it of that piquancy that strikes us so forcibly in the present view. The analysis might be pushed further, to the consideration of the effect of removing dormers, changing the style of chimney tops, etc.; but we have said enough to show what

" Great effects from little causes flow."

ACCOMMODATION.—The internal arrangements of this dwelling are so plainly exhibited on the plan of principal floor, fig. 1 , as scarcely to need explanation. G is an open entrance porch. A, 8 by 16 feet, is the entrance hall, and contains a flight of stairs. B, 16 by 18 feet, is the dining-room, lighted by a recessed twin window, and having an ample china closet attached. The parlor C, 16 by 16 feet, has a nice bay-window, but would be improved by a window extending to the floor on the side next to the entrance porch, an idea not fully conveyed by the engraving. The kitchen D, 16 by 16 feet, is well lighted, and provided with sink, side entrance, and small closet. Adjoining the kitchen there is a wash-house, 11 by 12 feet, and beyond this a wood-house or pump-room F, 7 by 12 feet, having outdoor communication independent of the kitchen.

Ascending to the second floor, fig. 2 we find the stair landing, marked by the letter H, from which we have ready access to the chambers I and J, and to the bed-room K and bath-room L. The chambers, as will be seen, are all furnished with good closets.

CONSTRUCTION.—A very pretty effect would be secured by building this cottage of wood, the weather-boarding being put on in the vertical manner, and the joints battened after one of the methods explained at fig. 8. The gable and eave cornice should be cut from 3-inch plank, in a bold manner, and also the ornament against the base of the pinnacles.

ESTIMATE.—Built of wood, in the manner above described, the cost of this design would not vary much from $4000, where timber is plenty; built of stone, and the walls furred inside for plastering, $650 should be added.

Samuel Sloan, HOMESTEAD ARCHITECTURE, 1861

1—PRINCIPAL FLOOR.　　　　**2—SECOND FLOOR.**

THE plan of this building was designed according to a ground plan by Mr. Huber, conveyancer, and is arranged with reference to economy and comfort. It contains fine halls in the first and second stories, with two comfortable rooms in the third story, and four rooms on the second and first stories, so arranged that they are placed conveniently with each other. It will make a roomy and cheap house, which would cost, if built of pointed-rubble masonry, in Philadelphia or vicinity, $7500.

The roof will be covered by ornamental-formed slates, with a flat tin roof on top, which answers as an observatory. Included in the estimate are the baths, water-closets, gas pipes throughout, low-down grates, marbelized-slate mantels in two rooms, sink, range, and a heater in the cellar; also, all modern improvements,—speaking-tubes, bells, etc.

First Floor.—1, front porch; 2, sitting-room, 15 by 18 feet; 3, hall, 7 feet; 4, parlor, 17 by 18 feet; 5, pantry, 6 by 8 feet 6 inches; 6, dining-room, 13 by 20 feet; 7, kitchen, 13 by 15 feet; 8, 9, closets.

Second Floor.—10, hall, 7 feet; 11, chamber, 15 by 18 feet; 12, chamber, 17 by 18 feet; 13, chamber, 13 by 20 feet; 14, chamber, 13 by 15 feet; 15, bath-room, 7 feet 6 inches by 8 feet 6 inches; 16, 17, 18, 19, closets.

A Country Residence

Isaac H. Hobbs, HOBBS'S ARCHITECTURE, 1876

FIRST FLOOR.   SECOND FLOOR.

H.W. Cleveland, William & Samuel D. Backus, VILLAGE AND FARM COTTAGES, 1856

Cottage

Wood
8 × 11

P

3 × 7
C

Kitchen

10 × 13

Sitting Room

9 × 10

Parlor

10 × 15

FIRST FLOOR PLAN
reversed

Bedroom
10 × 15

Bedroom
10 × 15

SECOND FLOOR PLAN

The vignette represents a study for a simple cottage, designed as a residence for men employed on the farm and in other operations about the estate. The cottage is in full view from the principal drive-road, and it therefore seemed worth while to consider it as an accessory in the landscape as well as a convenient home for those who were to live in it. The other side of the house showing the veranda would probably have offered a more picturesque view, but the vignette will serve to give a general idea of the simple effect aimed at. The basement, entered from a door on the outside, as shown on the sketch, was designed to be fitted up, for the use of the family, as a wash-room, and to be provided with drying-closet, ironing-room, etc. The principal floor explains itself, the two bedrooms below being for the housekeeper's use, and the chamber plan above, containing three roomy bedrooms, being set apart for the use of the men. Such a cottage, with the basement finished off, should cost about $1400 or $1500. In this instance the outlay was increased, from various causes, to $1800.

A Farm Cottage

Calvert Vaux, VILLAS AND COTTAGES, 1857

PLAN OF PRINCIPAL FLOOR.

Country House For Any Climate

Samuel Sloan, HOMESTEAD ARCHITECTURE, 1861

A LITTLE examination into the merits of this design, as illustrated by the engravings of elevation and ground-plans, will satisfy any one that our title, if not entirely elegant, has not been chosen without some attention to the correctness of its application. While we are well aware that it is next to impossible to prepare plans embracing all the conditions made imperative by a great diversity of climate, we are not less sensible that compromises can be effected, greatly extending the application of a given plan with but a limited amount of local modifications. To the Southern projector who may conceive a partiality for the idea here illustrated, we would say, give outside blinds and umbrage to all the windows, and build a detached kitchen, and you have a complete Southern house for a family of moderate size. The through hall, which effectually cuts off the dining apartment from the parlor and library, is a very liberal arrangement for a house of this size; and indeed this circumstance, combined with its peculiar application in the plan before us, is the basis of the compromise here intended between the varieties of climate.

ACCOMMODATION.—The hall A, fig. 2, entered from a neat front veranda, is 9 feet wide, and contains the principal staircase. The parlor B is 16 by 22 feet. By opening the sliding doors, the eye is greeted by the pleasing view of an octagonal bay-window; this is an appendage to the apartment C, a room 16 feet square, which would make a delightful sitting-room or library, according to the choice of the occupants. The dining-room D has two snug little china closets. The kitchen E, 14 by 10 feet, has a closet and flight of private stairs. On the second floor, fig. 3, we find three good chambers, F, provided with closets, and two smaller ones, H and G, the latter entered from the private stairs.

CONSTRUCTION.—Brick, stone, or wood are equally applicable to construction of this dwelling. If ordinary bricks or rubble-stone are used, it should be stuccoed; if built of wood, the framing should be boarded in the horizontal manner, the angles or corner posts being cased with vertical strips 5 or 6 inches wide, against which the abutting joint of the weatherboarding is made. A roof of shingles or slate is equally admissible, due provision having been made in the framing of the rafters for the greater weight of the latter. The execution of the joinery with well selected and seasoned wood, say white pine or cypress doors and dressings, yellow pine stairs with walnut hand-rail, etc., would be a satisfactory mode of internal finish.

ESTIMATE.—We put the cost of this, under the most favorable circumstances, at $4300.

1

2
PRINCIPAL FLOOR.

3
SECOND FLOOR.

A.J. Downing & Calvert Vaux, VILLAS AND COTTAGES, 1857

A Symmetrical Country Home

PLAN OF PRINCIPAL FLOOR

CHAMBER PLAN

An Irregular Country House

Samuel Sloan, HOMESTEAD ARCHITECTURE, 1861

IRREGULAR in plan and general outline, yet neat and chaste in detail, the design before us is a fair type of the beauty that may be attained without a tendency to extravagance in the exterior adornment of an edifice springing from an irregular basis.

ACCOMMODATION.—By a reference to fig. 2 , the plan of first floor, the internal arrangements will be perceived almost at a glance. A through hall B is entered from the piazza A. This hall contains the stairs, and affords access, by a side passage, to the kitchen E. The parlor C is 15 by 30 feet, and has a rectangular bay-window, communicating by a lengthened window with the veranda I. The dining-room D has also a bay-window, seen in the perspective view, which, by the way, is reversed from the plan. F is the butler's pantry, G a wood-shed, and H a kitchen closet.

The plan of the second floor exhibits the arrangement of the chambers. K is the landing of the stairs in the front building, from which the three chambers L are entered, and from which also the stairs are continued to the roof-story, in which three very comfortable bed-rooms may be fitted up.

A passage from the half-landing of the stairs leads to the bath-room M and the adjoining bed-room N, over the kitchen.

1 CHAMBER FLOOR

This house could be very efficiently warmed by a single furnace, the proximity of the flues being quite favorable to that mode: the hall, parlor, and dining-room, and the three chambers over, could all be kept comfortably warm, as the central position of the flues involves but little loss of heat.

CONSTRUCTION.—This design admits with equal facility the use of wood or more solid materials. The thickness of walls, as drawn, indicates the use of stone, which, in many districts, is the cheapest material. The pitch of the roof seems to demand shingle or slate; the drawing represents them of varied form.

ESTIMATE.—Built of stone and rough-cast in a neat, careful manner, and all the workmanship substantial and well finished, the cost of this house, in Pennsylvania or Ohio, will not vary much from $4600.

2

PRINCIPAL FLOOR.

An Artist's Studio & Cottage

The vignette illustrates an artist's studio, designed for Mr. Jervis M'Entee, landscape painter, of Rondout, and built by him of wood, fitted in a substantial, simple way, for $400. It is finely placed on an elevated site, and commands an extended view of the Kaatskills and the Hudson. On the plan it is one simple room: the ceiling line follows the line of the roof and collar beams, so as to give height and a more airy effect to the interior. All the rafters are left visible, the plastering being fitted between them. Some time after the design had been built and occupied, Mr. M'Entee added a portion of a simple cottage residence in corresponding style, the studio still remaining in use for its original purpose. The complete effect aimed at is shown on the lower view and plan.

As the parlor, the veranda, and the porch are not yet built, a somewhat disproportioned result is obtained *for the present*, as the wing looks larger than the house; but its accommodation and cost, as it stands, is all sufficient for the immediate needs and circumstances of its proprietor, who has judiciously preferred to run the gauntlet of his neighbors' criticism for a time, and to plan his house as he *will* want it, carrying it out by degrees as opportunity offers, rather than to adopt a snug arrangement complete in itself, which, although suitable enough for to-day, would, in all probability, be in a few years inconveniently small for his own needs; and if he wanted to sell at any time, could hardly fail to prove an undesirable investment on a site constantly improving in value, and that might, in all probability, be disposed of to advantage at any time, with a roomy house on it, or a building that could easily be made a good family residence, without pulling down the existing building or injuring its general appearance. The house as it at present stands, with hall, dining-room, pantry, small bedroom, and studio, on principal floor, three bedrooms and a little bath-room above, and basement kitchen, with cellars below, has cost $2000; and Mr. M'Entee calculates that another $1000 would render it complete, as shown, giving a second kitchen below, a best parlor and a best bedroom over, in addition to the accommodation already provided.

DESIGN FOR AN ARTIST'S STUDIO.

PLAN OF PRINCIPAL FLOOR.

N.E. VIEW.

SHOWING THE COTTAGE COMPLETED.

Calvert Vaux, VILLAS AND COTTAGES, 1857

THIS design is quite perfect in its plan, and contains all the requirements for internal comforts, as well as considerable exterior attraction. It is of a style which is much used, and its beauty will depend upon the proportion of its parts, and the correctness of its details. Cost, with all improvements, $8000.

Many mechanics throughout the country imagine that they can adopt what appears to them as beautiful in one house, and by transferring (or rather *apparently* transferring) it to their own, produce the same effect. Persons are continually sacrificing style, finish, and proportion in their buildings, in order to save architects' fees. We have buildings adjacent to Philadelphia that will sell for three times their cost; and there are many which have been built without the aid of an architect that will not realize their cost.

First Floor.—A, parlor, 13 by 30 feet 3 inches; B, hall, 13 by 13 feet; C, sitting-room, 13 by 16 feet 9 inches; D, dining-room, 12 by 24 feet 6 inches; E, kitchen, 11 feet 6 inches by 16 feet; F, scullery, 8 feet 9 inches by 14 feet; G, H, porches.

Second Floor.—I, chamber, 15 feet 10 inches by 11 feet 8 inches; J, chamber, 16 feet 10 inches by 13 feet; K, chamber, 13 feet 8 inches by 13 feet; L, chamber, 12 by 20 feet; M, chamber, 11 feet 3 inches by 16 feet 8 inches.

A Village Residence

Isaac H. Hobbs, HOBBS'S ARCHITECTURE, 1876

FIRST FLOOR.

SECOND FLOOR.

A Village House

HOW TO BUILD, FURNISH & DECORATE, 1883

A, front veranda, 10x16; B, hall, 7x20, C, parlor, 12x18, with bay window, 4x9, D, dining-room, 15x20; E, library, 12x15, with square bay window, 4x8; F, kitchen, 11x12; G, pantry, 8x8, H, store-room, 10x12; I, coal-room, 7½x8; K, wash-room, 7½x8; L, veranda, 8x16; M, veranda, 4x30, N, cistern, 9 feet diameter: O, well; c, c, closets; s, s, shelves; b, bath f, back stairs t, sink p, pump. Second floor:—hall, 7 feet wide, C, C, C, C, closets D, linen closet; E, attic stairs; F, servants' bed-room, 11x20, G, garret, B, bed-room, 15x15; H, bed-room, 12x15; K, bed-room, 12x18. Cost of this building £3,500.

FIRST FLOOR.   SECOND FLOOR.

Cottage

PANTRY   PORCH

CL

DINING ROOM
11'·0" x 12'·6"

KITCHEN
12'·6" x 12'·6"

PARLOR
12'·0" x 13'·0"

PASSAGE

DOWN

HALL

PIAZZA

FIRST FLOOR.

CHAMBER
9'·6" x 11'·11"

CHAMBER
9'·0" x 12'·6"

CL

CL

HALL

DOWN

CHAMBER
10'·0" x 13'·0"

UP

CLOSET

SECOND FLOOR

George & Charles Palliser, MODEL HOMES, 1876

A Southern Cottage

THIS design is intended to be built of frame, and the roof to be shingled. It should stand at such a distance from the road as to afford sufficient space for ornamental shrubbery, walks, etc. The cost of the building should fall within the limits of four or five thousand dollars.

Upon the principal floor the porch gives access to the hall, which opens into the parlor and dining-room; the kitchen is well placed, and ample in size. The second floor contains a hall and three liberal-sized chambers.

First Floor.—1, porch; 2, hall, 10 feet 6 inches by 15 feet; 3, parlor, 12 feet 6 inches by 20 feet; 4, dining-room, 15 by 18 feet; 5, kitchen, 12 by 12 feet; 6, back porch.

Second Floor.—7, hall, 10 feet 6 inches by 15 feet; 8, chamber, 12 feet 6 inches by 20 feet; 9, chamber, 15 by 18 feet; 10, chamber, 12 by 12 feet.

A Southern Cottage

Isaac H. Hobbs, HOBBS'S ARCHITECTURE, 1876

FIRST FLOOR.   SECOND FLOOR.

THIS design is a plain and ordinary kind of building, simply having those necessary parts common to all houses, with a porch, bay-, and projecting window, with a hood projecting over a twin window in the front. The plan is so arranged as to give it the appearance of largeness. People who are not versed in the true principle of design think every part should be of equal beauty. If so, the design would be meagre. Some feature must be predominant and strong, and something must be weak, or such a result cannot be obtained. This house, built of frame, in very good style, will cost between $3000 and $4000, with marble mantels, heaters, bath, and closets. We have had many orders for full drawings and specifications, etc., for this house. They have all proved satisfactory. In some localities they cost much more than we here state—some as high as $8000, others at prices stated. All depends upon the elaborate work desired and the cost of materials constructed with.

First Floor.—A, hall, 6 feet wide; B, parlor, 15 by 23 feet 9 inches; C, sitting-room, 13 by 13 feet; D, dining-room, 15 by 21 feet; E, kitchen, 13 by 11 feet 9 inches; F, G, porches.

Second Floor.—H, chamber, 15 by 23 feet 9 inches; I, chamber, 13 by 13 feet; J, chamber, 15 by 21 feet; K, chamber, 13 by 14 feet 9 inches; L, hall, 6 feet wide.

A Village Residence

Isaac H. Hobbs, HOBBS'S ARCHITECTURE, 1876

FIRST FLOOR.

SECOND FLOOR.

Stable

1, Tool room.

2, Poultry room.

3, Cow stall.

4, Feed room.

Yard

a, Walk.

b, Stable path.

c, Lawn.

d, Shrubbery.

e, Flower bed.

f, Evergreen screen.

h, Clothes yard.

i, Fruit.

j, Vegetables.

g. Summer house.

k, Well.

l, Cow yard.

m. Poultry yard.

n, Piggery.

o, Manure pit.

H.W. Cleveland, William & Samuel D. Backus, VILLAGE AND FARM COTTAGES, 1856

SECOND FLOOR PLAN.

10.3 × 12   C C   8.9 × 9.6

10.3 × 12   C C   8.9 × 9.6

W.R
11.6 × 13

S
8 × 13

C   C

B.R
8 × 13

K.
13 × 14.7

P
13 × 18

H
8.6 × 13

FIRST STORY PLAN.

Cottage

v, Verandah.

H, Hall.

P, Parlor.

K, Kitchen.

B R, Bedroom.

s, Scullery.

w R, Wood room.

A Village Residence

J.J. Thomas, THE REGISTER OF RURAL AFFAIRS, 1865

The plans and view here given represent a residence erected some years ago in the village of Union Springs, N. Y. It is built of wood, with the walls filled in with brick.

The plans need but little explanation. A double door, (the outer a Venetian blind,) leads from the parlor to the veranda, in front of the ornamental garden, and commanding a view of Cayuga lake, half a mile distant. The nursery contains a series of drawers, set even with the wall, for containing miscellaneous articles. They are nineteen in number and placed in five series, one above another, the upper ones being small and the lower ones large. The bed-room between nursery and kitchen may be used as a bath-room, being readily accessible to the kitchen for obtaining heated water. The walls of the pantry are furnished with continuous shelves, all of which are closed with tight, narrow doors. A door about two feet square, breast high, between the dining-room and pantry, having a shelf a foot and a half wide on the pantry side, admits the free passage of dishes

Principal Floor.

without opening the common door. A similar one is placed in the second story, between the room over the dining-room and the room for domestics over the kitchen, and proves a great convenience.

The observatory, shown in the perspective view, commands an extensive prospect, including many miles of Cayuga lake, the surrounding country and distant blue hills.

The basement is finished with a smooth floor of hydraulic cement, and is divided by eight-inch partitions into three

Chamber Floor.

rooms, as shown in the annexed plan. The outer one contains a stone cistern about six by ten feet, from which the water is drawn through an inclined pipe by a pump in the kitchen placed over a stone sink. The same room is also used as a coal-cellar, and contains the hot-air furnace. Adjoining this is a room for the general purposes of a cellar. It contains a set of hanging

Basement

shelves, a safe for articles of food, tight boxes for vegetables, &c., the latter being packed in fine damp moss. The third apartment is the fruit room, about twelve by twenty-eight feet. The shelves for containing the fruit are five and a half feet wide, and extend nearly the whole length of the apartment. The lower shelf is a foot from the floor, the other two with spaces of two feet between the shelves. The passage extending around allows free access for filling, picking over and selecting. The upper shelf being in a warmer stratum of air, should be furnished with lids to prevent evaporation and drying. Pears ripen finely on the lower shelves with a thick covering of woolen blankets.

This house stands on a small farm of about sixty acres, on one of the outer streets of the village, and the adjacent grounds of about two acres are represented in the annexed engraving. L is the carriage entrance from

the street, K the entrance to the farm and barns. R represents the ornamental garden, consisting of a closely shaved turf, through which the curved walk passes, and in which circular and irregular flower-beds are cut. Seats are placed under the trees and a summer-house in the remote corner.

In the rear of this portion, and separated by an evergreen screen is the kitchen and fruit garden *n*, containing rows of dwarf apples, dwarf pears, and the smaller fruits, so arranged that the cultivation can be performed to a considerable extent by a horse. A natural depression at *o*, about thirty feet in diameter and eight feet deep, with a curved walk to the bottom, is planted as a secluded flower-garden. On the other side of the dwelling *a*, and nearly hidden by trees, are the smoke-house *c*, the ice-house *d*, the children's play-room and tool-house *b*, and between them a group of bee-hives. The road *i*, extends to the carriage-shed *f*, and the horse-barn *e*, and *h h* to the orchard and farm—*g* represents the farm-barn.

The residence here represented, (built and occupied by the author of the REGISTER,) was erected when materials were cheap, at a cost of a little over three thousand dollars. At the present increased prices nearly double this sum would be required.

LANDSCAPING
◆ ◆ ◆

J.J. Thomas, THE REGISTER OF RURAL AFFAIRS, 1873

THERE ARE MANY FARMERS who desire to have their grounds about the dwelling laid out with some taste, but who cannot afford to keep up gravel walks, or to mow their lawns once a week. They would like a simple plan admitting the planting of shade trees, and the grazing of the grass by sheep or other animals, in lieu of mowing. Fig. 1 is intended to represent such a place, the entrance road having sufficient curve to remove all stiffness, and yet not so much as to give it a pretentious appearance. The common farm road lies on the left of these ornamental or shaded grounds, and both enter the yard devoted to the farm buildings at the rear.

A more finished plan is shown by fig. 2, where the carriage-way has more curve, passes by the front entrance, and before entering the rear grounds, has a place for the turn of carriages. The lawn may be kept

Fig. 1.—*Simple Plan of Farm Grounds.*

mowed, or be grazed short, as the owner may prefer. If mowed, a considerable portion of the small shrubbery may be planted near the dwelling, as shown in the plan; but if grazed, none but very large shrubs or small trees should be admitted. In planting the trees the owner will, of course, vary the places of the groups or belts, so as to have the most pleasing distant views open, and exclude any object of an undesirable or unsightly character. The farm road may lie at either side of these grounds, and is not shown in the engraving.

When the extent of ground devoted to ornamental planting is more limited, and means and time are at command to give it a handsome finish, it may be laid out as represented in fig. 3. A neatly made carriage way passes to the front entrance, and to the yard in the rear, and also turns in front for return. The circular beds on the left are for bedding plants, such as verbenas, pelargoniums, salvias, &c., or they may be occupied with tulips and other bulbs, or with annuals or perennials. In the direction of the barnyard, fruit trees may be planted, which should be of such symmetrical kinds as the more regular-growing varieties of the cherry and pear, which will flourish better than most other fruit trees when growing in grass.

For a small village lot which is too narrow to admit any breadth of lawn, and where **a small grass plot** is desirable, the plan shown in fig. 4

is particularly recommended. The dwelling is placed next the boundary, so as to give as much space as possible in the opposite direction. Beds for ornamental plants are in front of the bay window ; large shrubs or small trees are placed as shown in the plan, but no large trees should be admitted.

Towards the kitchen garden in the rear, a few of the

Fig. 2.—*Simple Grounds without Flower Garden.*

KITCHEN GARDEN

BARN YARD

Fig. 3.—*Finished Grounds of Country Place.*

more symmetrically-growing pear and cherry trees are planted. The walk is simple, but curved enough to remove all appearance of stiffness. In so small a plan everything should be kept in perfect neatness, as there is no excuse for neglect.

A large village lot, or a

small place in the country, may be laid out as in fig. 5, where the carriage road enters on the left, and the foot walk on the right. A group of circular flower beds fronts the bay window at the side, and a few are placed still farther off, on the opposite side of the walk.

GARDEN

Where the owner has a horse which he may employ in cultivating his garden, much labor will be saved by laying the ground out in lines running in one direction only, so that the horse may freely pass from one end to the other, leaving a grass strip vacant about 10 or 12 feet wide to turn upon, as in fig. 6. Rows of small dwarf apples, (worked on Paradise stock,) dwarf pears, raspberries, grapes, gooseberries, currants, &c., are placed at intervals of 12 feet or more, (15 or 20 feet would be better,) between which all the large vegetables are planted, so as to allow horse cultivation.

Fig. 4.—*Plan of Small Lot.*

For the first mellowing, a light one-horse steel plow does well —after which a fine tooth one-horse harrow answers an admirable purpose, provided it is passed so often as to keep the

Fig. 5.—*Large Village Lot.*　　　　　Fig. 6.

ground constantly clean and mellow, before the weeds can get their puny heads above ground. When long neglected, and after the weeds have grown half a foot, it then becomes necessary to use the plow again ; and it is in consequence of this neglected management that horse cultivation is objected to, as making rough and imperfect work. Those portions of soil which lie in the rows, and which the harrow cannot reach, must, of course, be worked over with the common or pronged hoe. When onions, beets, &c., are sown in rows a foot or a foot and a half apart, a very narrow cul-

Fig. 7.

Fig. 8.

tivator, or what is better, one with a tooth taken out, so as to go over a row and take two spaces at a time, is a great saver of labor. The man who does this horse cultivation must know how to do it neatly and carefully, and not be a bungler.

When all the heavy work is done by hand-spading, the garden may be laid out as in fig. 7, a dial or pillar for a flower-pot occupying the centre, from which alleys pass off in four directions to the alley which goes around the whole—currant bushes, grapes, &c., lining the fence or wall. A more ornamental form is shown in fig. 8, where a greater number of alleys radiate from the centre, which may be a handsome flower bed, with a few curved flower beds adjoining, the rest being fruits and vegetables. Where the garden is large enough, an additional alley may pass through the central parts lengthwise with the garden.

Fig. 9.

FLOWER BEDS.—These sometimes have a rough and crude appearance, because they are not laid out and finished with care and precision. For general purposes we prefer the circle to all other forms of flower beds when cut in grass. This is easily made of any desired dimensions, and by grouping the circles together, almost any required ornamental effect may be produced, (fig. 9.) In fig. 10 we have represented a symmetrical figure of seven circles, the larger in the centre, and arranged at equal distances from each other. This regular grouping is well adapted to any formal position in the grounds, near the dwelling, under a bay window, &c. The effect may be modified by taking only three contiguous circles in a triangle, three in a row, four in a rhomboidal position, or any other arrangement. Single circles may be scattered anywhere in the

Fig. 10.

Fig. 11.

grounds, along the walk as may be desired, and can scarcely ever be out of place. After the plants and shrubs have grown to some height, the outline of the bed may be marked again distinctly when it needs a new dressing, by the contrivance shown in fig. 11, where a is a central stake, b the arm of any required length, and c the rod for scratching. This may be used on all beds of equal size, and may be adapted to any other by boring holes in the arm.

A good effect is produced in front of a window or veranda by the series of elliptical beds shown in fig. 12. These may be longer and narrower, so as to present an appearance like radiating beds. The elliptical form is more difficult to draw than the circle, but the operation may be performed as shown in

Fig. 12.

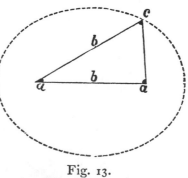

Fig. 13.

fig. 13—two stakes being driven at $a\ a$; throwing over these stakes the looped cord b, which connects the three points $a\ a\ c$, and a marking stick, c, placed within it and moved around, scratches the ellipse as shown by the dotted lines. By lengthening or shortening the cord loop, and changing the distance of the two stakes, figures of any size or elongation may be readily drawn.

A four-sided bed of a more fanciful form may be made as shown in fig. 14, by first drawing the circle represented by the dotted line, dividing it into four parts,

Fig. 14.

and completing the figure by describing halves of circles from centers on these lines where they cross the circle, for the outside, and on centres half way between for the inside circle. A six-sided figure may be similarly drawn by dividing the circle into six parts at *a a a*, and again at the intermediate points, fig. 15. The appearance of such a bed when planted is shown by fig. 16.

Fig. 15.

Fig. 16.

The arabesque form, figs. 17 and 18, should be sparingly introduced into any garden, as it not only requires a good eye in laying out, but in preserving the outline in after years. The form is given and the curves made by the mode figured and described on page 292, volume IV, RURAL AFFAIRS, Nearly, if not quite as ornamental an effect is given by the grouping of circles as already described. The arabesque forms

Fig. 17.

Fig. 18.

require at all times the highest finish to the grounds, for nothing can appear worse than an attempt at high ornament with failure from a want of neat and finished keeping.

It was formerly the practice to form edgings of box plants, but the stiff-

Fig. 19.—*Section of Circular Flower Bed, bordered with hard brick set on end beneath the surface.*

ness of appearance which these produce has led to their disuse. Besides, when beds are cut in turf, but little edging is needed other than the neatly trimmed turf which surrounds them. As it is difficult, however, to keep the turf edge mathematically even, without some guide, it answers a good purpose to place a line of *hard burnt* brick on end just beneath the surface of the soil, as shown in fig. 19. If the soil is well underdrained, these will keep their place a long time, and serve as an accurate guide for the workman as he trims the curved border of the bed with his spade.

Fig. 20.—*Brick Border inclining inward.*

These bricks are placed so as to incline slightly outward at the top; but another, and in some respects a better mode is to give the inclination shown in fig. 20, so that the end of the bricks shall form an inclined, smooth circular surface, and make the bed slightly lower than the grass. The brick, pointing inward, may be thus made to fit closely together when they are seen above ground.

◆ ◆ ◆

Ornamental Planting

A.J. Downing, LANDSCAPE GARDENING, 1841

J.J. Thomas, REGISTER OF RURAL AFFAIRS, 1860

OUNTRY homes are of two kinds—the repulsive and the beautiful. The former are occupied by those who know nothing of domestic enjoyment, and who seek happiness in the barroom and grog-shop. They never see any charms in the works of nature—ornamental shrubbery to them is "brush," and flowers are only "weeds." They never plant a rosebush nor a shade tree. They sometimes set out a few apple and cherry trees. But these are left to take care of themselves, and what remain after ten years, appear like those shown in figure 1, instead of attaining the perfection seen in figure 2, as

Fig. 1.

Fig. 2.

they would have done if well managed and properly cultivated. They have an especial contempt for all ornamental trees, and exclaim,

Fig. 3—*Premises of the Man "who Cares nothing for Looks" nor for the Comforts of Home.*

"What! set out trees that don't bear anything fit to eat—that are only good to look at!" Their dwellings are bleak and desolate. There is nothing about them attractive to their children, who grow up with no attachment to home, and with little appreciation of the social virtues. The first figure on this page, (fig. 3,) is a representation of all that is inviting in the homes of their childhood, and where from the earliest

Fig. 4—*Premises of the Man who makes Home attractive to his Children.*

dawn of their forming minds, they have received most of their impressions of life. Few of them have been able to surmount these discouraging influences, and they have become coarse and unintelligent. How different might have been their character if they had been brought up under the influences of the other home represented on the same page!

This neat cottage (fig. 4) cost no more in the first place than the dilapidated one. Its owner kept it in perfect repair, and planted and cultivated the encircling grounds during those spare moments that his neighbor who lives in the other, occupied at the tavern. Each house cost nearly a thousand dollars in building; while the planting and cultivation of the grounds about the latter, did not require an expenditure of fifty dollars.

There is now scarcely an intelligent mind who does not admit for the above reasons, the real and substantial value and utility of ornamental planting. Added to its utility, is the fascinating employment of imitating the most beautiful natural groupings of objects, by planting and arranging trees. With all these inducements, great and increased attention should be given to the subject, and it would open a world of exalted enjoyment to those who pursue it. Most fortunately, it does not require necessarily a profuse expenditure of money. As much skill may be employed in decorating the limited grounds of a cottage, at an expense within fifty dollars, as in laying out and planting a magnificent park of hundreds of acres, costing many ten thousands.

Much money is wasted in attempts to ornament the grounds of a dwelling before a well digested plan has been adopted. Alterations alone have sometimes cost more than the execution of a complete well arranged design. We have known owners to expend more in excavating and in building terraces, with a real injury in appearance, than others would in effecting the most finished improvement. In one instance the owner of a suburban residence, with the constant labor of two gardeners, succeeded in accomplishing less in the way of neat and beautiful appearance, than another with the services of a single gardener but two days in each week. The art of ornamental planting cannot be learned in a single day, but like any other art, requires much thought and study, with all the assistance that may be derived from the experience of others. Those who wish to understand the subject completely are referred to Downing, Sargent, and Kemp, for full instructions; but a short article like this may perhaps afford many useful hints to those who cannot give so much time to the subject, or whose moderate grounds and limited means may not warrant great expenditure.

In offering suggestions on this subject, it will be best to begin at the beginning, and lay down briefly a few rules for selecting a site for a dwelling. The following requisites may be regarded as important nearly in the order in which they are named, but some will transpose them more or less, according to their preferences.

1. Healthfulness.
2. Neighborhood.
3. Soil and climate.
4. Suitable site, convenience of access, &c.
5. Scenery and views.

The first is all-important, as no home comforts can atone for ruined health. The second is scarcely inferior, for a family possessing civilization and refinement cannot properly enjoy themselves when constantly exposed to the petty annoyances of vulgar and pilfering neighbors, and who are shut out entirely from the social enjoyment of such as are of a congenial character. Where a whole neighborhood unites in works for public benefit and moral improvement, the very atmosphere seems purer and more delightful, than where semi-barbarism and selfishness are the ruling influences. A *fertile soil* is all-essential to the resident who would obtain the necessaries and comforts of life from his own land; and a climate favorable to the cultivation of the finer fruits is equally so to every one who expects to enjoy a constant circle of these most wholesome and delicious luxuries. The *site*, and suitable conveniences for access, are important considerations. A low, foggy place, will be unhealthful; a high one, without shelter, will be bleak and cold; if very near a public road, it will be exposed to noise, dust, and obtrusive observation; if remote from the road, much needless traveling will be required, and not a little inconvenience will be found in time of deep snows. A gentle eminence, and a moderate distance from the public road, and the shelter of evergreens on the side of prevailing winds, will obviate most of these difficulties. A quiet side-road branching from a main highway, will often be better than directly on a great thoroughfare. Comparative nearness to places of public worship, to schools, a post-office, mill and railroad station, are each of considerable importance, and should all be taken into consideration. The value of *fine scenery* will be variously estimated; some would prize it as all-essential, while others would scarcely think of it. Some would merely covet a showy situation as seen from the nearest highway, in order to draw the admiration of travelers; others, discarding such motives, would only desire beautiful views from the windows of the dwelling or from the surrounding grounds, in order to make their homes interesting and attractive to their children.

The site having been selected, the next step is to build the house. This portion of labor does not belong to our present subject, but the plan and intentions should be well understood before the exact spot for the house is fixed upon, and its frontings determined. This precaution is essential in order to secure the finest views, and to furnish protection from winds, or from undesirable odors or unsightly objects.

Great progress has been made within a few years in the art of ornamental planting, but it is still so common to witness defects, that to point out some of these defects in the first place, will more fitly prepare the way for specific directions.

The most common error of past years, but now rapidly disappearing, is the practice of planting only in straight lines or geometric figures. Absolute stiffness reigned supreme, in the attempt to avoid any approach towards *irregularity.* A neighbor, intelligent in other things, when he saw the first specimen of the natural mode of planting, exclaimed, "Why, Mr. T.! you have none of your trees in rows!" He considered a want of straight lines a striking evidence of a bungler. The geometric style not only required this formal regularity, but *symmetry,* as it was termed, demanded that every object should have its corresponding one. A tree on one side must oppose just such a tree on the other side; a row on the right was to have its accompanying row on the left. It is stated that the old gardener of the Earl of Selkirk, was so strongly imbued with this mania for symmetry, that when he shut up the thief who stole his fruit in one summer-house, he was compelled for the sake of symmetry, to put his own son in the other opposite. How immeasurably more pleasing and beautiful than this stiff and artificial mode, is the simple imitation of the beautiful and picturesque in nature, which constitutes the modern or natural style of planting.

It is not an unfrequent error to suppose that the modern style consists *merely* in *irregularity.* But irregularity without arrangement, is not taste—confusion is not the beautiful in nature. The *perfection* of art consists in producing a pleasing effect, while the art which produced it is concealed from the eye of the spectator. The scenery which artificial planting produces, may *appear* to be the accidental arrangement of agreeable parts or objects; but it must really be the result of close study and a careful eye—in the same way that the roughly dashed work of a skillful painter, where every touch, rude and accidental as it may seem at first glance, is found on taking the whole together, to produce a most perfect and complete combination of different parts. And one great excellence of the modern style consists in its complete adaptation to all grades of residences—it does not require costly embellishments, nor a profuse outlay—the cottage resident may show as much skill in a *tasteful simplicity,* as the owner of the magnificent park in the disposition of his broad lawns and majestic forest trees.

In order to produce the best effect in grouping trees, these requisites are essential—*unity, harmony,* and *variety.* The following is an example

Fig. 5—*Example in Grouping.*

in illustration (fig. 5)—and the scene represented in fig. 6 on the following page, exhibiting a natural group of elms, possesses everything agreeable

Fig. 6—*Grouping Elms.*

but *variety*—and it possesses much of this quality so far as the arrangement of the trees is concerned, but it lacks variety from the trees being
all of one kind.   For this reason the preceding example (fig. 5) is free
from objection.

The next figure (fig. 7) affords an illustration of monotonous irregularity; and presents the same appearance that some grounds do after
they have grown up with trees which have been planted all over
without regard to effect or to open portions of lawn, or distant views

Fig. 7—*Monotonous Grouping.*

towards beautiful objects.   On the other hand, the two following figures
present fine examples of natural grouping; the first (fig. 8) exhibiting
the advantage which may be taken of slight undulations in the ground,
in increasing the picturesque variety which it may afford; and the second
(fig. 9) a fine and exceedingly varied sky outline produced by a group of
dissimilar trees, yet all supporting each other and harmonizing together.

No error is more common with those who have "a *little* knowledge"
on the subject of planting and designing grounds, than in attempting to
combine within the limits of a small place, all the different objects that

Fig. 8.

can be introduced only in extensive grounds. Neat and harmonious simplicity is sacrificed to incongruous confusion. This propensity is

Fig. 9.

sarcastically exhibited by Lowell in his account of the "*Rural Cot of Mr. Knott,*" a dwelling

> "'Twixt twelve feet square of garden plot,
>   And twelve feet more of lawn,"

containing meadow and upland, a water view, (consisting of pump and trough,) and a woodland made up of

> "Three pines stuck up askew,
>   Two dead ones and a live one."

The house was built cheaply of wood, and painted in imitation of stone; but so much was expended on odd conceits and flimsy ornaments, that

> "Ere many days poor Knott began
>   Perforce accepting draughts that ran
>   All ways—except up chimney;

> The house, though painted stone to mock,
> With nice white lines round every block,
>   Some trepidation stood in,
> When tempests (with petrific shock,
> So to speak,) made it really rock,
>   Though not a whit less wooden."

Among other errors often committed in the attempt to crowd many objects within a small space, is the construction of a multiplicity of walks, beyond what is useful or essential; planting trees over the whole surface, rendering the grounds uniformly spotted with them; introducing too many flower beds; making artificial mounds or terraces, instead of merely softening off the naturally varying surface; placing rustic objects in immediate connection with the house, the architecture of which does not at all harmonize with them; and especially to be avoided is the error of introducing *shams*, which will be discarded by every person of correct taste. Among these, as Kemp observes, are " artificial ruins, mere fronts to buildings, bridges that have no meaning, and for which there is no necessity," to which we may add all puny attempts at artificial rock work, which are only small heaps of stones.

Persons of more moderate pretensions, including a large portion of such as live on medium-sized farms, fall into another error. They devote to ornamental planting a square plot of ground exactly in front of the dwelling, and varying from half an acre down to two rods square. This is

FERGUSON, ALBANY

Fig. 10—*Residence with a Neat Front Yard only.*

enclosed with a picket fence in the form of a *tight pen*, with one straight walk passing through the center from the front door down to a small gate opening into the public highway. Very few ever pass through this gate or enter through the front door; but carriages, wagons, and foot passengers go in at the large gate just without this square yard, and enter the house by a side or back door. The square yard is therefore often allowed to grow up with grass or weeds, and is shaded by a few cherry trees, one or two lilac bushes, and a few hollyhocks. Occasionally it is seen in much better order, with a straight and neatly-kept gravel walk lined with shrubs and flowers, and with rows of cherry and pear trees on either side—(fig. 10.) This is, however, the only neat portion of the whole premises; for the worm-fence enclosures on the right and left, and the back yard, contain a numerous collection of cord-wood, old rails, empty boxes, barrels and barrel hoops, unburned brush, plows and sleds, wagons and carts, pails and kettles, chips, slop puddles, &c. It appears, however, like a neat and comfortable residence to the traveler who is careful to look at it only at the moment when he is exactly in front.

Plans of Grounds

A small town or village residence, with only a few feet of ground, may be laid out as represented in the accompanying figures. Fig. 11 exhibits

Fig. 11.

a front yard about twice the breadth of the house, and with about fifteen or twenty feet from the front door to the street. Instead of the straight narrow walk too often seen, this is broad, with curved sides, passing on the left

to the garden, and on the right to the kitchen and barn. A small gate on the right admits entrance to the kitchen without passing up the front walk, and the curved passage from this side-gate being closely planted with evergreens, is rendered less conspicuous. Fig. 12 is a larger place, admitting greater variety in the form of the walks, and several arabesque flower beds cut in the smooth shaven lawn. The exterior is planted with the larger shrubbery or trees, evergreens standing nearest the boundary, and growing thickly where it is desired to conceal any unsightly neighboring building or other undesirable

Fig. 12.

object, and leaving an opening where the view is of a pleasing character. In grounds of the limited extent of these two residences, perfect neatness should prevail; the soil should have been previously made deep and rich, that the trees and shrubs may grow freely with rich foliage; the part covered with grass should be smooth, (the grass seed having been sown very thickly, or at the rate of two or three bushels per acre,) and the grass mowed twice a week within half an inch of the surface, during the early part of the season, and once a week later; the gravel walk should be as smooth as a floor, slightly convex or curved upwards, and trimmed with a true curve at the edges.

Fig. 13 exhibits a plan for the grounds of a village residence, varying from half an acre to an acre, and where a horse and cow are kept. The front portion, as far back as the dwelling, is occupied with lawn, kept

closely shaven, with trees and shrubs, and a few flower-beds bordering the walks. In the rear and on the left is a small orchard, through which the carraige road passes; and in the yard which it enters is the horse and carriage barn, the cow-house, and poultry-house. On the right is the fruit and kitchen garden. This is laid out so as to admit of plowing at least once a year, as well as horse-cultivation so far as may be desired. The rows of fruit trees are dwarfs, with currants and gooseberries and the other smaller fruits. The boundary of the kitchen garden is planted with roses and flowering shrubs, through which a neatly kept walk passes, thus giving the advantages of a wider extent of ornamental grounds. Converting the

13— *Grounds of a Village Residence.* kitchen garden into a lawn, and providing a kitchen garden by extending the grounds to the left, would form a more perfect place.

A design for the grounds of a farm residence, where half an acre to an acre is devoted to ornamental planting, is exhibited in fig. 14. The carriage road enters nearly in front of the house, bending slightly, and forming a sweep for turning—from this the carriage may return to the road, or pass to the carriage-house in front of the barn-yard. On the left is a pear and cherry orchard planted in the quincunx manner; in front and to the right is the lawn, kept smoothly shaven and planted with trees and shrubs. These grounds are traversed by a curved walk five

Fig. 14.

and a-half feet wide, which is bordered with several flower-beds. The boundaries are most thickly planted where the view is undesirable beyond; and the view across the lawn is left nearly unobstructed towards the most distant points, and especially towards the seat *a*, and the summer-house *b*. In the rear of the grounds is the garden, which combines the kitchen and fruit garden for dwarf trees. They are planted in rows, and consist of dwarf pears, dwarf apples on doucain stock, gooseberries, currants and raspberries, and dwarf plums. Between these rows the ground is cultivated by horses, the garden vegetables being planted in drills to admit the passage of a narrow cultivator.

DESIGN FOR A FOUNTAIN.   DESIGN FOR A WELL-HOUSE.

George E. & F.W. Woodward, ARCHITECTURE, LANDSCAPE GARDENING AND RURAL ART, 1867

Trees

J.J. Thomas, REGISTER OF RURAL AFFAIRS, 1860

THE BALDNESS OF NEW PLACES.—The remorseless manner in which the native trees have been totally cleared away from country residences, has left most of them in a very bleak and unsheltered situation. A neighbor had a fine natural oak grove before his house, but being strongly imbued with the cut-and-slash mania, chopped them all down, and then planted a row of maples in their place, which would require about thirty years to attain the size of the oaks. Sir Joshua Reynolds said he would paint Folly in the shape of a boy climbing over a high fence with an open gate close at his side. He might have done it more effectually by representing an American land-owner cutting down all his native shade trees, that he might enjoy transplanted ones thirty years afterwards.

There are, however, many places where a thin natural growth of trees may be found, and among which a residence may be built. Yet with a most singular fatuity, such land-owners avoid these beautiful natural parks, and build in an open field adjacent. We witness frequent instances of this folly.

Where trees have grown up thinly, their heads have become rounded and well developed, and nothing is easier than to remove those possessing the least beauty, or which may stand in the range of fine landscape views. Even such as have grown closely together, and have shot up bare trunks, may be greatly improved in appearance in a few years, by heading them down soon after thinning out, as low as a good supply of side branches will admit, and gradually bringing them down into a fine form in successive years. The addition of other trees by planting, will soon greatly improve the appearance of the whole, and impart to the wildness and crudeness of nature, the grace and finish of an embellished landscape.

Where necessity leads to the selection of such places as have no trees, the most rapid mode of supplying the deficiency is, first to prepare the soil in the best manner by trenching or deep subsoiling, at the same time working in large quantities of old manure or compost. Then plant moderate-sized, thrifty trees, which have been carefully taken up, and keep the soil bare and mellow for a few years, foregoing the pleasure of a green turf for the sake of a more rapid growth of the trees. Large trees when set out present a more conspicuous appearance at first, and some may be interspersed, but in a short period the smaller ones will have outstripped them, and will then present a richer, more dense, and far more beautiful foliage. By selecting a portion of the most rapidly-growing sorts, as the Silver Maple, the European Larch, and the Abele, among deciduous trees; and the Norway Spruce, Scotch Pine and Austrian Pine, among evergreens, a more speedy effect will be secured.

GARDENING

◆ ◆ ◆

I'll relate an incident connected with cottage gardening that may interest if it does not benefit some of those into whose hands this book may fall. About a dozen years ago I had the pleasure of making the acquaintance of a gentleman whose duties compelled him to be at his desk in a close office in the City of New York, from 9 o'clock A. M. to 4 P. M. Being naturally of a weak constitution, his sedentary life soon made him the victim of dyspepsia to such a degree that he felt that he must soon resign his situation. He was then a man of forty, entirely ignorant of anything pertaining to country life, and it was with great misgivings and reluctance that, by the advice of his physician, he changed his home from a closely built part of New York to a cottage in the then country-like suburb of Bergen Heights, N. J. His means enabled him to purchase a modest cottage built on a lot 50 by 150 feet ; he did not want the land, he said, but the cottage was such as he fancied, and the ground had to go with it. It was about this time that I formed his acquaintance, through some business transaction, and he asked my professional advice as to what he could do with his land, which he had already begun to consider somewhat of an incumbrance. I replied to him that, if I was not greatly mistaken, in his little plot of ground lay a cure for all his bodily ills, and that besides it could add to the comforts if not the luxuries of his table if he would only work it. "I work it !" he exclaimed. "You don't suppose that these hands could dig or delve," holding up his thin and bloodless fingers, "and if they could I know nothing about gardening." I told him I thought neither objection insurmountable if he once begun.

The result of our conversation was, that he resolved to try, and try he did to a purpose. Our interview was in March, and before the end of April he had his lot all nicely dug over, the labor being done by his own hands during an hour and a half each morning. His custom was to get up at six o'clock and work at his garden until half past seven. This gave him ample time to dress, get breakfast, and be at his desk in the city by nine. The labor of merely digging was (to him) heavy and rather monotonous, but he stuck to it bravely, and when he again presented himself before me for plants and seeds and information as to what to do with them, it was with some pride that I saw my prescription had worked so well, for my friend then looked more like a farmer than a pallid clerk. The regulating of his little garden was a simple matter, and was done according to the following diagram :

1

Cauliflower, cabbage and lettuce.	Strawberries.
Cucumbers, onions, and parsley.	Raspberries.
Beets, carrots, and parsnips.	Tomatoes.
Bush beans.	Asparagus and Rhubarb.

During his first season, of course, he made some blunders and some failures, but his interest in the work increased year by year. His family was supplied with an abundance of all the fresh vegetables and fruits his limited space could admit of being grown—a supply that it would have taken at least $150 to purchase at retail, and stale at that. But the benefit derived from the cultivation of this cottage garden was health—strong, rugged health—that for the six years he was my neighbor, never once failed him.

I know this case is an extremely exceptional one, for I never knew another man who so resolutely worked himself into health. There are hundreds of business men, book-keepers, salesmen, clerks, and the like who live in the suburbs of all great cities, many of whom can ill afford to pay for the keeping of the plots surrounding their cottages, but who think they can far less afford to do the work themselves. As a consequence, in nine cases out of ten, the rear, at least, of their suburban plots is a wilderness of weeds. But this is not the least of the evils, the owner has a certain amount of muscular force, and this, be it more or less, being unused, its possessor pays the penalty of his laziness in dyspepsia, and a host of other ills. The proofs are apparent everywhere that garden operations are conducive to health and longevity. The work is not unduly laborious, and when fairly entered into has a never-failing interest. The growing and the watching of the great variety of plants gives a healthy tone to the mind, while the physical labor demanded by cultivation takes care of the body.

Peter Henderson, GARDENING FOR PLEASURE, 1875

Garden Implements

The tool-shed is an important and necessary append-age to a well kept garden. The following list includes such implements as are generally needed in private gardens :

THE WHEELBARROW, (Fig. 2).—The wheelbarrow is

Fig. 2.—GARDEN WHEELBARROW.

an important vehicle in the garden, for the moving of soils, carrying manures, and for conveying the products of the vegetable garden to the house or place of storage, and numerous other purposes. It may be purchased of different sizes and styles, or can be "home-made" by those possessing a little mechanical skill.

THE SPADE, (Fig. 3).—The uses of the spade in a garden are too obvious, and general, to need description. The best in use are Ames' cast-steel, which are light, strong, and durable, and work clean and bright.

THE SHOVEL, (Fig. 4).—The shovel is used for load-ing, and for mixing and spreading composts and short manures. They are made with long or short handles.

THE DIGGING FORK, (Fig. 5), or Forking Spade, is used instead of a spade to dig in manures, to loosen the earth about the roots of trees, or for taking up root crops ; being less liable to cut or injure them than the spade. It is often

Fig. 3. Fig. 4. Fig. 5. Fig. 6. Fig. 7. Fig. 8.

used instead of the spade, as by its aid the soil can be more readily broken and pulverized.

THE MANURE FORK, (Fig. 6).—Is made of cast-steel with from four to six prongs, and is used for mixing, loading, and spreading manures, work which could not be efficiently done without it.

THE COMMON OR DRAW HOE.—There are several patterns of draw hoes, but the one in general use is the common square hoe, as represented in fig. 7. Its uses in the garden are manifold, and it has frequently to do duty for several other implements. Its principle uses are to clean the surface of the ground from weeds, to open trenches for seeds, and to cover them.

THE PRONG HOE, (Fig. 8).—This is one of the most useful of all garden tools, and is far superior to the blade hoe for stirring and pulverizing the soil. It cannot, it is true, be used where weeds have been allowed to grow to any considerable hight, but then we claim that in all well regulated gardens, weeds should never be allowed to grow so large that they cannot be destroyed by the prong hoe.

THE DUTCH OR PUSH HOE, (Fig. 9), is sometimes preferred to the preceding for cutting the weeds be-tween the rows of vege-tables, a work which can be done very quickly by its aid ;

Fig. 9. Fig. 10. Fig. 11. Fig. 12. Fig. 13.

it is not so generally useful as the draw hoe, but is better for the special purposes of destroying weeds.

THE REEL AND LINE, (Fig. 10), are necessary in every well regulated garden, enabling us to plant in straight and accurate rows. The line should be of strong hemp, and is wound upon the reel when not in use.

THE PRUNING SAW, (Fig. 11), is used for cutting off branches that are too large for the knife, for removing dead ones, etc. It can be had in various sizes, from fourteen to twenty inches in length.

THE GARDEN TROWEL, (Fig. 12), is used for setting the smaller kinds of plants when transferred from pots to the open ground ; for transplanting annuals and many other uses, it is a very necessary little implement.

PRUNING AND BUDDING KNIVES, (Fig. 13), are ne-cessary to every gardener. They are of different sizes and shapes, for the various purposes of grafting, bud-ding, etc., and are made of the best steel.

GRAPE SCISSORS.—These are slender-pointed scissors, used for thinning out the berries of foreign grapes when

Fig. 14.—LAWN SCYTHE.

they are about half grown, so that those that are left may have room to develop. This operation should never

Peter Henderson. GARDENING FOR PLEASURE, 1875

be neglected if large berries and well shaped bunches are desired.

FLOWER GATHERERS.—A very useful article; the scissors cutting off, and at the same time holding fast the flower or fruit after it is cut, thus enabling one to reach much farther.

LAWN SCYTHES, (Fig. 14).—The lawn scythe is now but little used, the lawn mower taking its place, unless on hill-sides or among trees or shrubs, where the lawn mower cannot be worked.

LAWN MOWERS, (Fig. 15).—The great improvements made in Lawn Mowers during the past few years, and the low price at which they may now be obtained, have made their introduction common to every garden. They are of many sizes, from the small machine that can be easily worked by a boy,

Fig. 15.—LAWN MOWER.

and admirably adapted for city garden plots, to the large horse mowers, that may be daily seen in use in our larger parks. We have in use both the "Excelsior" and "Archimedean" Lawn Mowers, and have found them excellent in all respects.

THE GARDEN ROLLER, (Fig. 16), is indispensable to a well kept lawn, and should always follow after mowing, keeping the ground level and compact; and after gravel walks have been raked over, the roller is necessary to smooth them down.

THE WOODEN LAWN RAKE, (Fig. 17), is used for raking off lawns previous to and after using the scythe or lawn mower, and for removing dead

Fig. 16.—ROLLER. leaves and other rubbish.

THE RAKE, (Fig. 18), is used to level the surface of the ground after it has been spaded or hoed, and to prepare it for the reception of seeds or plants. Rakes are made of different sizes, for convenience in using between rows of plants, with from six to sixteen teeth. When a crop like cabbages is newly planted, we use the rake in preference to anything else, as raking over the surface before the weeds start to grow, destroys the germ of the weed, never allowing it to appear at all.

THE GRASS EDGING KNIFE, (Fig. 19), is used for cutting the grass edgings of flower-beds, its rounded edge fitting into curved lines, for which the spade would be unsuitable.

Fig. 17.   Fig. 18.   Fig. 20.   Fig. 21.   Fig. 22.

Fig. 19.

THE SICKLE, (Fig. 20).—This is a most useful implement for switching around and trimming off grass, in places where the scythe or lawn mower cannot be used, or where the place to be cut is small.

HEDGE SHEARS, (Fig. 21), are better fitted for clip-

A.J. Downing, THE HORTICULTURIST, 1846

Dwarf Pear Tree

ping hedges than the Bill Hook, sometimes used for the purpose, particularly in inexperienced hands. A line should be set at the hight to which the hedge is to be cut, as a guide to work by.

HAND-PRUNING SHEARS, (Fig. 22). —These are very efficient and useful; they will cut off a small branch as clean as if a knife had been used. They are indispensable in pruning small fruit-trees and vines, and for use in the grapery and garden.

POLE OR TREE PRUNING SHEARS, (Fig. 23). — These shears are attached to a pole, and operated by means of a lever moved by a cord or a wire; they enable one to cut off branches from trees, shrubbery, etc., that are beyond the reach of the ordinary pruning shears. Branches of an inch and a half in diameter may be easily cut off with this instrument.

Fig. 23.—TREE PRUNER.

GARDEN SYRINGE, (Fig. 24).—The syringe is in

Fig. 24.—GARDEN SYRINGE.

daily use in the greenhouse or conservatory, where syringing is necessary to keep the plants in a flourishing and healthy condition. They are made of several sizes and patterns, and fitted with roses for dispersing water with varying force.

WATERING-POT.—A watering-pot is indispensable in the greenhouse or conservatory, where it is daily needed. It should be obtained of a suitable size, from one to four gallons, with a rose for sprinkling, which may be detached at will.

THE EXCELSIOR PUMP, (Fig. 25), is a very compact and useful implement for greenhouse and garden work. It is easily operated, and throws a continuous stream. It is very effective for watering shrubbery, gardens, or lawns, and may be used in an emergency as a fire extinguisher and prevent a conflagration.

Fig. 25.—EXCELSIOR PUMP.

THE SIDNEY SEED-SOWER, (Fig. 26).—This is a very useful implement, enabling

Fig. 26.

Fig. 27.

Fig. 31.

small frame covered with a pane of glass, are very useful, but as they exclude some light they are not equal to those made with glass all around. Hand-glasses with metal frames and glass sides and top, are made of different sizes and styles, one of the more elaborate of which is shown in fig. 31. Though somewhat expensive, they will, if carefully used, last many years.

Trellises, or supports for plants, are needed in the flower and vegetable garden not only for climbers, but for keeping plants which have weak stems within proper bounds. Trellises for pots may be purchased ready-made, as may those for climbing roses and such plants; they are usually made of rattan upon a frame of light wooden stakes, and some are made entirely of wire. A person of a mechanical turn can readily make all that will be needed.

Fig. 32.

Fig. 28.

the operator to sow seeds with perfect regularity, especially in wet or windy weather. It will distribute large or small seeds with equal regularity, either broadcast or in drills or pots.

THE EXCELSIOR WEEDING HOOK, (Fig. 27), is a very handy implement for removing weeds from among small and tender plants, and for stirring up the soil. It can be used between rows of seedlings, ornamental plants, or wherever it is desirable to remove weeds, without injury to the plants or soiling the hands.

Fig. 29.—SMALL GARDEN SET.

NOYES' HAND WEEDER, (Fig. 28), is a kind of miniature hand hoe, and is very convenient and useful for working between plants, dressing pots, and cleaning away weeds, where a large hoe could not be used to good advantage.

LADIES' AND CHILDRENS' GARDEN TOOLS, (Fig. 29).—In all flower gardens there is a great deal of hand-work to be done. This lot of small implements consisting of a spade, fork, rake, and hoe, will be found very useful in working on small flower borders.

Fig. 30.—STEP LADDER.

STEP LADDERS, (Fig. 30).—The step-ladder is always useful in a garden, especially during the fruiting season. It is made in different sizes, varying from three to ten feet, and weighing from ten to thirty pounds; it is made with flat steps, so that a person may stand upon them while working, and can be extended or contracted as required. For use amongst large trees, in the orchard, a much greater length of ladder is required, and there are various forms of orchard ladders in use, but the step-ladder is sufficient for all ordinary garden uses.

HAND-GLASSES.—The uses of these have been mentioned under cauliflowers, cucumber, etc. Home-made hand-glasses, being simply a

A few engravings are given here as suggestions. Fig. 32 shows a useful support made with a barrel hoop and staves; the same plan may be carried out with two or more hoops, and laths, if staves are too heavy. This will answer for tomatoes, raspberries, and various other plants. A more permanent tomato trellis is shown in fig. 33, in which slats are supported by Λ shaped uprights. If put together with screws, such a trellis may be carefully put away in the fall

Fig. 33.—TOMATO TRELLIS.

and made to last several years. A rustic trellis, like that in fig. 34, is often useful in the flower garden, or it may serve when covered with climbers to divide the flower from the vegetable garden. It is made of sticks of cedar or other durable wood, set as shown in the engraving, and tied where the bars cross one another with strong tarred twine. With these examples

Fig. 34.—RUSTIC TRELLIS.

as suggestions, one will find no difficulty in making more elaborate supports and with other materials.

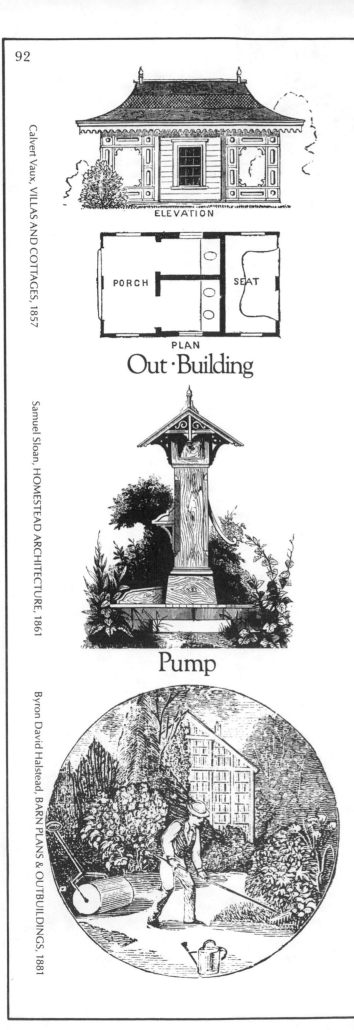

Calvert Vaux, VILLAS AND COTTAGES, 1857

ELEVATION

PORCH SEAT

PLAN

Out·Building

Samuel Sloan, HOMESTEAD ARCHITECTURE, 1861

Pump

Byron David Halstead, BARN PLANS & OUTBUILDINGS, 1881

George E. & F.W. Woodward, ARCHITECTURE, LANDSCAPE GARDENING AND RURAL ART, 1867

A Tool House, Etc.

COMPOST TANK 8 × 6

GARDEN TOOLS 7 × 9

W. C. 6 × 6

PLAN.

OUT·BUILDINGS
•••

SQUIRE SLIPSHOD'S BARN.

FARMER THRIFTY'S BARN, AS SEEN IN WINTER FROM HIS BACK DOOR.

J.J. Thomas, THE REGISTER OF RURAL AFFAIRS, 1859

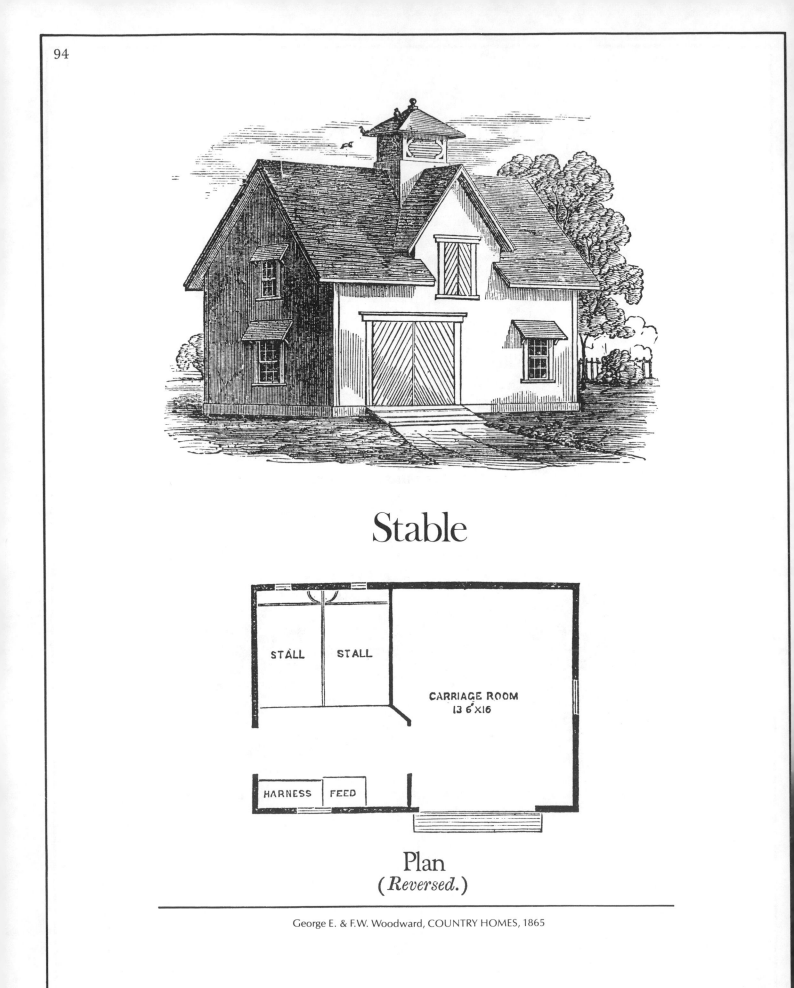

Stable

STALL   STALL

CARRIAGE ROOM
13 6'×16

HARNESS | FEED

Plan
(Reversed.)

George E. & F.W. Woodward, COUNTRY HOMES, 1865

Stable

Plan

George E. & F.W. Woodward, COUNTRY HOMES, 1865

Ice House

It is only within a few years that ice, in all seasons, has been classed among the necessaries of life. In large cities it is indispensable, but the cool spring-house or cellar in the country impresses many with the idea that ice, in summer months, can only be regarded as a luxury. Along with other conveniences in keeping with this progressive age, the ice-house has its place, and a country-seat of any pretensions is not complete without it.

It is simple in construction, and can be built very cheaply of rough materials, or made as elaborate as is desirable. It forms a pretty feature about the grounds, if treated with some architectural taste.

George E. & F.W. Woodward, COUNTRY HOMES, 1865

18 X 12

ENCLOSURE

Plan

George E. & F.W. Woodward, COUNTRY HOMES, 1865

Plan

Cottage Stable

STALL

11'6" X 24

STALL   CARRIAGE ROOM

16 X 20

Byron David Halstead, BARN PLANS & OUTBUILDINGS, 1881

George E. & F.W. Woodward, GRAPERIES AND HORTICULTURAL BUILDINGS, 1865

Green House

Fig. 1 is a perspective view of the house. The west end is boarded and battened. This corresponds with the general design of the house, and presents a neat finish. The sides, except the potting room, are of glass, the sashes being about three feet high. Every other sash is hung at the bottom, for the purpose of ventilation. The roof is a continuous glazed roof, and is quite flat, which is a decided advantage to the plants within. There are no ventilators in the roof, the top ventilation being effected by means of the sashes over the doors at each end, which are hung at the bottom for this purpose, and afford abundant ventilation for a house the length of this one. There is an ornamental crest along the ridge, and at each end a neat finial.

2 – *Ground Plan.*

George E. & F.W. Woodward, COUNTRY HOMES, 1865

Stable

This stable may be constructed either of wood, or of stone. It contains stalls for four horses, and affords space for their accomodation, together with a harness room and a tool closet. This latter is a convenience very essential to the comfort of the owner, as well as to the proper care and preservation of such implements as belong especially to the carriage house and stable.

This building should be surrounded and screened with fruit trees and shrubbery, and then, with its evident architectural effects, it will become an attractive feature in the landscape of which it becomes a part, with the other accessories of the elegant country home.

FEED SHOOTS

COACH R.
27 X 30.

TOOL C.
9'6"X10

HARNESS R.
5 6 X 10 6

Plan

GARDEN SEAT.

SUMMER. HOUSE.

Garden Improvements

A.J. Bicknell, WOODEN & BRICK BUILDINGS, 1875

WELL HOUSE.

ICE HOUSE.

OUT. HOUSE.

SCALE TO ELEVATIONS. — PLANS ONE HALF.

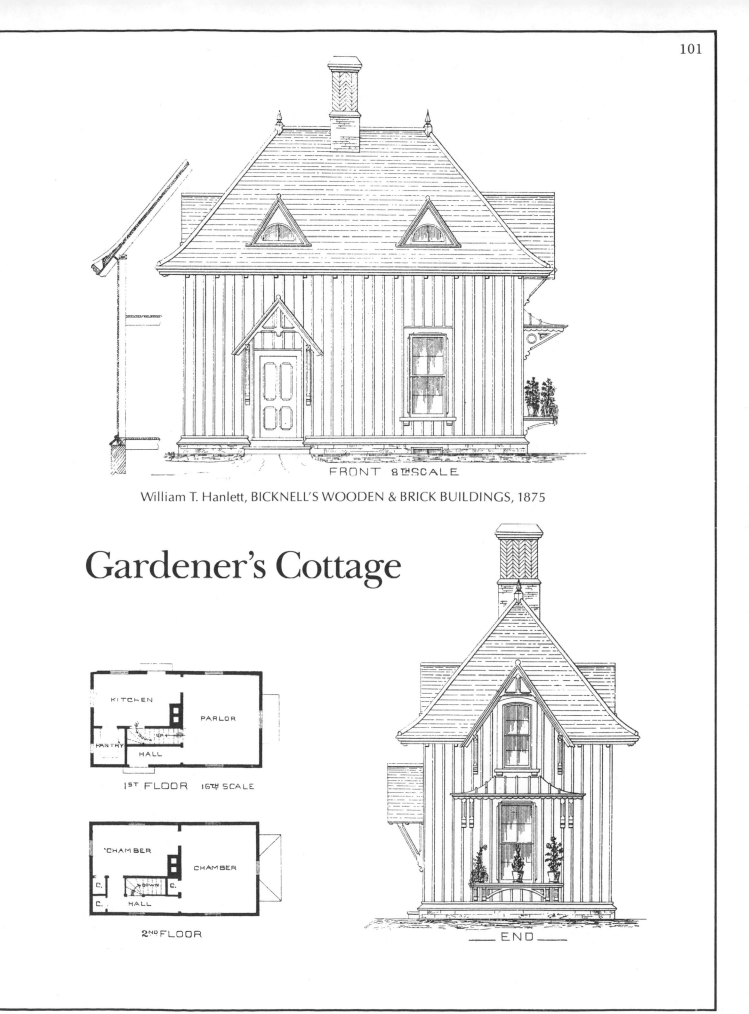

FRONT 8TH SCALE

William T. Hanlett, BICKNELL'S WOODEN & BRICK BUILDINGS, 1875

Gardener's Cottage

KITCHEN

PARLOR

PANTRY

DOWN UP

HALL

1ST FLOOR 16TH SCALE

'CHAMBER

CHAMBER

C.

DOWN

C.

C.

HALL

2ND FLOOR

END

Out·Building Details

FINIAL AT "A".

VANE AT "B".

"A"

"B"

VENTILATOR FRONT.

VENTILATOR.

SECTION ON LINE "A" "B".

"D"

"D"

VENTILATOR SIDE.

CARRIAGE HOUSE DORMER.

STABLE DOOR.

Deck plate. 4 x 8

GUTTER

plate. 4 x 6

girth. 4 x 8

joist. 4 x 8

sill. 4 x 8

SECTION OF MAIN WALL.

Sawed work

BRACKET AT K.

PLATFORM BRACKET AT "N".

Sawed work

SECTION MAIN DORMER.

END OF OPEN SHED.

PLAIN DORMER.

K

K

N

N

DORMER HAY DOOR AND PLATFORM.

doors 2'0" x 6'0"

MAIN DORMER.

C

OPEN SHED ARCHES.

PLATE 4 x 6

SECTION ON LINE "C" "D".

DESIGN FOR AN ICE HOUSE.

12' x 12' inside

S. Sawdust 12" space

A. Air space 8" space

S

A

A

S

doors

D

ELEVATION

PLAN.

A.J. Bicknell, WOODEN & BRICK BUILDINGS, 1875

BUILDING DETAILS

♦ ♦ ♦

WOODEN CORNICES.

ELEVATION.   SECTION.   ELEVATION.   SECTION.

BRACKET.   BRACKET.

RAFTERS and SCROLLS.

RAILINGS.

A.J. Bicknell, WOODEN & BRICK BUILDINGS, 1875

Details

GUTTER.

BRICK WALL.

SECTION OF CORNICE.

PLAIN CORNICE FOR A MANSARD ROOF.

SECTION OF DECK MOULDING

SECTION OF CORNICE.

GUTTER

CAP AT B.

CORNICE AND BRACKET.

BALCONY. WITH SAWED AND CHAMPFERED WORK.

PLAIN BALCONY.

SECTION.

CAP AT A.

GABLE ON BRACKETS. SAWED WORK

GABLE ON BRACKETS. SAWED AND CHAMPFERED WORK.

SECTION.

BRACKET.

BRACKET.

G.E.HARNEY ARCHITECT 149 B'WAY. N.Y.

PLAIN VERANDA. END.

SECTION.

FRONT.

VERANDA. SAWED AND CHAMPFERED WORK. END

FRONT.

G.E. Harney, BICKNELL'S WOODEN & BRICK BUILDINGS, 1875

¼ INCH TO THE FOOT.

ENLARGED DETAILS 1 INCH TO THE FOOT.

Details

Verandas and Porches

SECTION AT P.

SECTION AT R.

P.

R.

BALUSTER.

SECTION AT A.

A.

CAPITAL AT C.

C.

George E. Woodward & E.G. Thompson, WOODWARD'S NATIONAL ARCHITECT, 1868

SCALE. ½ Inch to One Foot:

EXTENSION CORNICE.

MAIN CORNICE.

ANGLE CREST.

Details
WOODWARD'S NATIONAL ARCHITECT,
1868

FRONT
CHAMBER WINDOW.

FRONT
HALL WINDOW.

PEDIMENTS.

FRONT VERANDA.

REAR PIAZZA.

FRONT DOORS.

ENLARGED DETAILS ½ INCH TO THE FOOT.

SECTION ON B C.

SECTION ON D E.

FINIAL AND CRESTING AT F.

SECTION ON K L.

Details

GABLE FINISH, AND WOOD AND
IRON FINIALS AND CRESTING.

¼ Inch to One Foot.

FIGURE AT G.
⅛ FULL SIZE.

FINIAL AT H.

FINIAL AT A.

FINIAL AT R. (ROUND)

FINIAL AT R. (SQUARE.)

SECTION ON M N.

Outside Color

We are not among those who cast off, and on a sudden condemn, as out of all good taste, the time-honored white house with its green blinds, often so tastefully gleaming out from beneath the shade of summer trees; nor do we doggedly adhere to it, except when in keeping, by contrast or otherwise, with everything around it. For a century past white has been the chief color of our wooden houses, and often so of brick ones, in the United States. This color has been supposed to be strong and durable, being composed chiefly of white lead; and as it *reflected* the rays of the sun instead of *absorbing* them, as some of the darker colors do, it was thus considered a better preserver of the weather-boarding from the cracks which the fervid heat of the sun is apt to make upon it, than the darker colors. White, consequently, has always been considered, until within a few years past, as a fitting and *tasteful* color for dwellings, both in town and country. A new school of *taste* in colors has risen, however, within a few years past, among us; about the same time, too, that the recent gingerbread and beadwork style of country building was introduced. And these were both, as all *new* things are apt to be, carried to extremes. Instead of *toning* down the glare of the white into some quiet, neutral shade, as a straw color; a drab of different hues — always an agreeable and appropriate color for a dwelling, particularly when the door and window casings are dressed with a deeper or lighter shade, as those shades predominate in the main body of the house; or a natural and soft *wood* color, which also may be of various shades; or even the warm russet hue of some of our rich stones — quite appropriate, too, as applied to wood, or bricks — the *fashion* must be followed without either rhyme or reason, and hundreds of our otherwise pretty and imposing country houses have been daubed over with the dirtiest, gloomiest pigment imaginable, making every habitation which it touched look more like a funeral appendage than a cheerful, life-enjoying home We candidly say that we have no sort of affection for such sooty daubs. The fashion which dictates them is a barbarous, false, and arbitrary fashion; void of all natural taste in its inception; and to one who has a cheerful, life-loving spirit about him, such colors have no more fitness on his dwelling or out-buildings, than a tomb would have in his lawn or dooryard.

Locality, amplitude of the buildings, the purpose to which they are applied — every consideration connected with them, in fact, should be consulted, as to color. Stone will give its own color; which, by the way, some prodigiously smart folks *paint*—quite as decorous or essential, as to "paint the lily." Brick sometimes must be painted, but it should be of a color in keeping with its character,— of substance and dignity; not a counterfeit of stone, or to cheat him who looks upon it into a belief that it may be marble, or other unfounded pretension. A *warm* russet is most appropriate for brick-work of any kind of color — the color of a russet apple, or undressed leather

Red and yellow are both too glaring, and slate, or lead colors too somber and cold. It is, in fact, a strong argument in favor of bricks in building, where they can be had as cheap as stone or wood, that any color can be given to them which the good taste of the builder may require, in addition to their durability, which, when made of good material, and properly burned, is quite equal to stone. In a wooden structure one may play with his fancy in the way of color, minding in the operation, that he does not play the mountebank, and like the clown in the circus, make his tattooed tenement the derision of men of correct taste, as the other does his burlesque visage the ridicule of his auditors.

A *wooden* country house, together with its out-buildings, should always be of a cheerful and softly-toned color — a color giving a feeling of warmth and comfort; nothing glaring or flashy about it. And yet, such buildings should not, in their color, any more than in their architecture, appear as if *imitating* either stone or brick. Wood, of itself, is light. One cannot build a *heavy* house of wood, as compared with brick or stone. Therefore all imitation or device which may lead to a belief that it may be other than what it really is, is nothing less than a fraud — not criminal, we admit, but none the less a fraud upon good taste and architectural truth.

It is true that in this country we cannot afford to place in stone and brick buildings those ornate trimmings and appendages which, perhaps, if economy were not to be consulted, might be more durably constructed of stone, but at an expense too great to be borne by those of moderate means. Yet it is not essential that such appendages should be of so expensive material. The very purposes to which they are applied, as a parapet, a railing, a balustrade, a portico, piazza, or porch; all these may be of wood, even when the material of the house *proper* is of the most durable kind; and by being painted in keeping with the building itself, produce a fine effect, and do no violence to good taste or the most fastidious propriety. They may be even sanded to a color, and grained, stained, or otherwise brought to an identity, almost, with the material of the house, and be quite proper, because they simply are *appendages* of convenience, necessity, or luxury, to the building itself, and may be taken away without injuring or without defacing the main structure. They are not a *material* part of the building itself, but reared for purposes which may be dispensed with. It is a matter of taste or preference, that they were either built there, or that they remain permanently afterward, and of consequence, proper that they be of wood. Yet they should not *imitate* stone or brick. They should still show that they *are* of wood, but in color and outside preservation denote that they are appendages to a *stone* or *brick* house, by complying with the proper shades in color which predominate in the building itself, and become their own subordinate character.

Not being a professional painter, or compounder of colors, we shall offer no receipts or specifics for painting or washing buildings. Climate affects the composition of both paints and washes, and those who are competent in this line, are the proper persons to dictate their various compositions; and we do but common justice to the skill and intelligence of our numerous mechanics, when we recommend to those who contemplate building, to apply forthwith to such as are masters of their trade for all the information they require on the various subjects connected with it. One who sets out to be his own architect, builder, and painter, is akin to the lawyer in the proverb, who has a fool for his client, when pleading his own case, and quite as apt to have quack in them all. Hints, general outlines, and oftentimes matters of detail in interior convenience, and many other minor affairs may be given by the proprietor, when he is neither a professional architect, mechanic, or even an amateur; but in all things affecting the *substantial* and important parts of his buildings, he should consult those who are proficient and experienced in the department on which he consults them. And it may perhaps be added that none *professing* to be such, are competent, unless well instructed, and whose labors have met the approbation of those competent to judge.

There is one kind of color, prevailing to a great extent in many parts of our country, particularly the northern and eastern, which, in its effect upon any one having an eye to a fitness of things in country buildings, is a monstrous perversion of good taste. That is the glaring red, made up of Venetian red, ochre, or Spanish brown, with doors and windows touched off with white. The only apology we have ever heard given for such a barbarism was, that it is a good, strong, and lasting color. We shall not go into an examination as to that fact, but simply answer, that if it be so, there are other colors, not more expensive, which are equally strong and durable, and infinitely more tasteful and fitting. There can be nothing less comporting with the simplicity of rural scenery, than a glaring red color on a building. It *connects* with nothing natural about it; it neither *fades* into any surrounding shade of soil or vegetation, and must of necessity, stand out in its own bold and unshrouded impudence, a perfect Ishmaelite in color, and a perversion of every thing harmonious in the design. We eschew *red*, therefore, from every thing in rural architecture.

Lewis F. Allen, RURAL ARCHITECTURE, 1862

Study For Cottage Roof Alteration

Calvert Vaux, VILLAS AND COTTAGES, 1857

A.J. Downing, THE HORTICULTURIST, 1846

VIEW OF A COMMON COUNTRY HOUSE.   1

Improving A Country Home

In *figure* 1, is seen a building that our readers will recognize at a glance, as the portrait of a plain country house, common in almost every neighborhood. Whilst there is perhaps nothing mean in the expression of this house, neither is there any thing in the least tasteful, or above the character of *common-place*. It belongs to the large class of dwellings whose presiding architectural genius is that of the "*bare and bald*."

In *figure* 2, is seen our proposed alteration and improvement of this house.

In the first place, to give spirit and character to it, we have boldly projected the roof, and ornamented the eaves. To give expression to the tame line of roof, we have added a small gable in front. The window pierced in this gable, will serve to light and render useful an additional room in the garret. For the meagre and insufficient porch, we have substituted a veranda ten feet wide, along the whole front; the shade and comfort of which in summer, makes it at least equal in value to any room in the house.

A part of the roof of this veranda, viz: that portion under the shadow of the gable, is finished with a tight sealed floor, so as to form an agreeable balcony to the central window of the front. The windows themselves, (though this is not so important,) we should prefer to change from the common form, to that of the more expressive and cottage-like *latticed sash*, as shown in the engraving.

We think no one can compare these two buildings without confessing that the alteration confers a character of taste and picturesqueness on what was before a very ordinary and insipid building. The improvement does not involve any material change in the body of the house itself, but merely in those external parts easily altered

2   VIEW OF THE SAME, IMPROVED

and added to.

Let us add a few words on the details themselves, that we may be the better understood. The roof should project two and a half feet all round the house. This projection is easily made by taking off the siding directly under the eaves of the old roof—introducing pieces of joists as rafters; upon which, carry out the rafter boarding, and piece out the roof to the necessary breadth.

The verge boards, or eave boards, (i. e. the ornamental piece running round below the outer edge of the roof,) must be cut out of sound *two inch* plank. It is the besetting architectural sin of half the carpenters in the country, (and more especially those in New-England,) to make these portions of a rural cottage of *thin boards*. Nothing gives a cottage, otherwise good, such a rickety, *paste-board-ish* air. The spirit of the carvings and ornaments of the gothic villa, of which these cottages are modified forms, is that of elegant solidity—not "*gingerbread*" flimsiness.

The supports of the veranda are simple solid posts or columns, six or eight inches in diameter, left square for base and capital, and hewn to an octagon in the shaft. The arch which runs at the top, from one to the other, is cut from two inch plank.

Nothing is heavier and less agreeable than the common square chimney. We would therefore advise the owner of *figure 1* to complete the alteration by adopting the simple form of carrying up distinct flues, standing on a common base, and connected at the top, as we have shown in *figure 2* The expense is but little more than in the common mode, and the effect far lighter and more agreeable.

ESTIMATE.—The cost of the proposed alteration of this house, will vary from $400 to $700. The cost of lumber and of the mechanic's labor, varies so widely in the different States, that it is impossible to give an estimate which will be an accurate one, for any two sections of the country. Where we write, the whole could be completed in a workmanlike manner, for about $550.

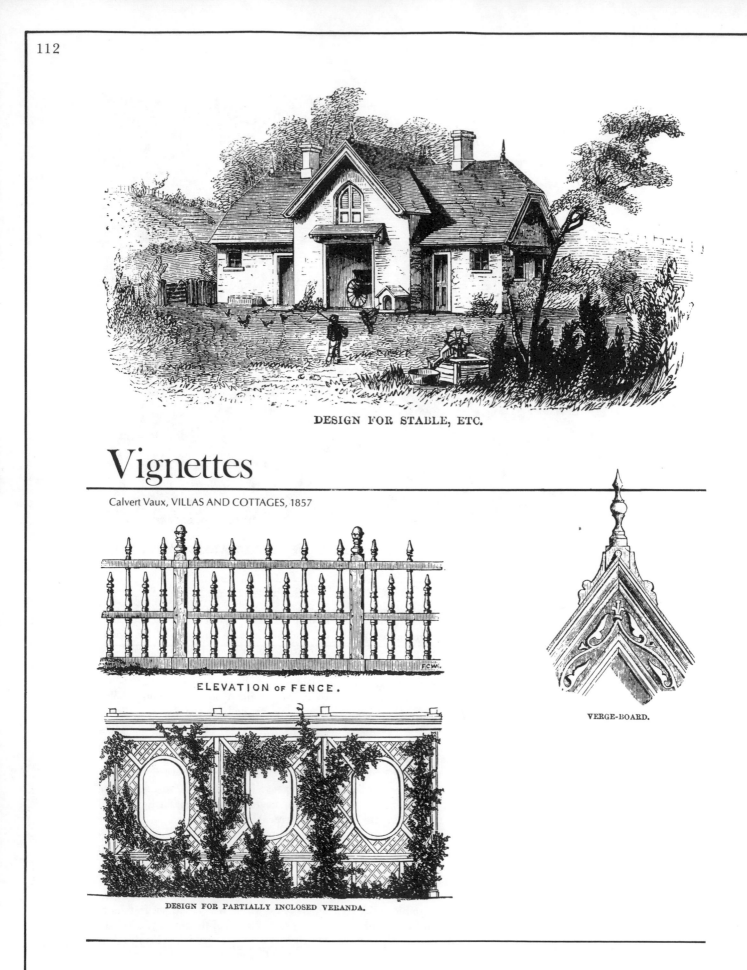

DESIGN FOR STABLE, ETC.

Vignettes

Calvert Vaux, VILLAS AND COTTAGES, 1857

ELEVATION OF FENCE.

DESIGN FOR PARTIALLY INCLOSED VERANDA.

VERGE-BOARD.

FURNISHINGS

• • •

Chamber Suite

CHAMBER SUITE No. 10.—From Warren Ward & Co.

This suite, made after Eastlake's designs, either in Ash or Black-Walnut, is very chaste and elegant, and is finished with either marble or wood tops. The pieces are : a Bedstead, French Dressing Bureau (French Plate Glass, 30 x 38), Washstand, Table, two Chairs, Rocker and Towel-Stand.

A.J. Bicknell, SPECIMEN BOOK OF ONE HUNDRED ARCHITECTURAL DESIGNS, 1878

Chamber Suite

CHAMBER SUITE NO. 9.—From Warren Ward & Co.

This is a very stylish suite, after English designs, made both in Ash and Black-Walnut, and composed of the same pieces as No. 10. This is made with the Dressing-Case as illustrated (size of glass, 20x44), and with the French Bureau.

A.J. Bicknell, SPECIMEN BOOK OF ONE HUNDRED ARCHITECTURAL DESIGNS, 1878

Cottage Furniture

Fig. 1.   *Fig.* 2.   *Fig.* 3.

Fig. 1. Is a small tea or work-table. The top is hinged on a triangular box, which may be used to hold work in. When not in use, the top is set up on edge, and when brought down it fastens with a common catch fastening.

Fig. 2. Is a neat work-table, which may be made by any joiner out of the common woods of the country, at a very trifling expense.

Fig. 3. Is a small dressing-table with a drawer in front, to hold combs, brushes, &c.

Fig. 4.   *Fig.* 5.

Fig. 4. Is a circular flower-stand.

Fig. 5. Is a small wash-hand-stand or table, in the Gothic style, with drawer, shelf, &c.

Fig. 6.   *Fig.* 7.

Fig. 6. Is a box footstool. The top is an outside frame, with webbing stretched across to support the stuffing above, which is covered with carpeting of the same kind as that of the floor of the room in which it is to be used. The sides are of wood, painted to match the other furniture.

Fig. 7. Is an extension table, with two folding leaves and two portable legs, unscrewed and taken off when the leaves are folded up.

Cottage Furniture

GODEY'S LADY'S BOOK, 1849

Fig. 1.

Fig. 2.

Fig. 3.

Fig. 1. A corner cupboard for glasses or china. It may also serve for a book-shelf, and the drawer for music or manuscripts.

Fig. 2. A plain wardrobe.

Fig. 3. A bureau book-case in the Gothic style.

KITCHEN SETTEE TABLE.
Gervase Wheeler, RURAL HOMES, 1851

SLOAN'S HOMESTEAD ARCHITECTURE, 1861

Chamber Furniture

This PLATE consists of a Suit of Chamber Furniture. The Bedstead is rounded at the foot, and the headboard is one large panel, veneered four different ways, with the grain crossed, to prevent its shrinking; the carving is just sufficient to carry out the design, and is well executed; the mouldings are all massive and well arranged.

The Wardrobe is in style to harmonize with the bedstead. It has mirror doors, and a separate lock on each door, leaving the door to close one inch on the center-piece; by this arrangement the door can shrink without leaving a crevice for dust to enter. The inside of the whole is grained to imitate maple, which makes a neat and clean finish.

The Dressing Bureau is of large size, with a marble top, and large mirror to swing in the standard. It is finished to match the other articles in the suit.

The Washstand is elliptical in front, with closets in the ends and drawer in the middle; it is open in the center, with marble top, and has marble in the opening, where there is sufficient room for the foot-urn.

The other articles required for a full suit are a lounge, a comfortable arm-chair, four or six chairs, a towel-stand, and most generally a small table. The space on the plate would not admit of them.

F.J.PILLINER.SC

SLOAN'S HOMESTEAD ARCHITECTURE, 1861

This PLATE represents a Suit of Plain Dining-room Furniture. The style is plain and economical. The Sideboard is four feet six inches long, and is finished with a white marble top. The Etagere top has two mirrors in the back, which give a good finish to it; the under part is divided into closets, with shelves; it has two drawers under the marble.

The Dining-table extends eight, ten, or twelve feet, according to the wants of a purchaser; it has a very neat appearance, and is a favorite for plain furnishing. A Case containing the loose leaves accompanies the table; the leaves are solid walnut or oak, as the wood happens to be wanted.

The Sofa is a comfortable lounging place, with spring-seat, and pillow-springs in the arms; it is covered with hair-cloth, morocco, worsted reps, or enameled oil-cloth.

The Chair is made either with stuffed or cane seat, and is a very substantial, plain article, which suits with the rest of the furniture.

Additional pieces can be ordered to match. A complete suit would also include a butler's tray, a side-table, and a pair of arm-chairs.

Plain Dining~room Furniture

Cottage Furniture

Fig. 1.

Fig. 2.

Fig. 1—Is a very convenient washstand, in high favor with the ladies. When not in use, the basin is concealed by two box covers, which are hinged, and which open and turn over when the stand is used, affording space for soap-holders, brush, trays, &c. There is a drawer below, with partitions for keeping these and various other articles belonging to the toilette ; one partition having a flat board raised two inches from the bottom of the drawer, and being pierced with holes for perfume bottles, &c. Below this drawer there is a deep cupboard with double doors.

Fig. 2—Is a table for invalids, commonly called a bed-table, which is a very great convenience in sickness. The top of this table is made to rise or fall at pleasure, by raising or lowering the upper part of the pillar *a*, which is perforated with holes at given distances, to admit the peg *c*, and which works in a square groove in the centre of the lower part.

Fig. 3.

Fig. 3. A strong chair put together with mortice and tenon.

Fig. 4.

Fig. 4. A comfortable easy chair, with stuffed sides and bottom, movable cushions and castors.

Fig. 5.

Fig. 5. Is a Gothic bench without arms or drawers, but with a paneled back and square legs.

Cottage Furniture

Fig. 1.   *Fig.* 2.

Fig. 1. Is a fixed corner cupboard in the Go-thic style, with glazed doors.

Fig. 2. Is a secretary and book-case, with a falling board, which serves as a writing-desk.

Fig. 3.

Fig. 3. Is a settle with drawers, often used in taverns. The back protects the sitter from the current of air from the door.

Fig. 4.

Fig. 4. Is a handsome Grecian bench, with turned legs.

Cottage Furniture

GODEY'S LADY'S BOOK, 1849

In the designs for cottage furniture, we furnish the cheapest and prettiest articles that can be manufactured. We wish to convince our readers that they can at the same time, with the aid of the patterns we give, combine utility, beauty and economy.

Fig. 1. A DRESSER. The middle drawer, which is drawn out, has a lift-out box or tray,

Fig. 1.

Fig. 2.

which is divided in the centre for knives, forks and spoons in daily use ; and underneath, in the bottom of the drawer, is a space for those not in use. The other two drawers are for clean table-cloths and towels. The cupboard in front is made in three panels, to look uniform ; but it has only two compartments, one for glasses and tea-cups and saucers, the other for fruits, sweet-meats, spices, &c.

Fig. 2. A dresser having beads on the edge to hold on the plates and dishes. The three draw-ers are for table-cloths, &c., as in *Fig.* 1, and the closets for corresponding purposes.

Fig. 3. A design for a sideboard in the Gothic style.

Fig. 4. The same open. The top compart-ment is for table-cloths, the others for table fur-niture.

Fig. 3.

Fig. 4.

CRANK HANDLE AND PORCELAIN KNOB.

PLAIN FACE LATCH.

ASTRAGAL FACE LATCH.

ESPAGNLETTE BOLT.

Cottage Hardware

The Baldwin & Many Co., New York

Gervase Wheeler, RURAL HOMES, 1851

HAT AND COAT HOOK.

SILVER PLATED GOTHIC FRONT DOOR BELL-PULL.

FRENCH WINDOW HINGE.   RABBETED LOCK.

BLIND OR DORMER WINDOW FASTENING.

SLOAN'S HOMESTEAD ARCHITECTURE, 1861

Dining~room Furniture

This PLATE represents a fine Suit of Dining-room Furniture. This is a favorite style, and the effect of the furniture in a room is much better than the plate represents.

The Buffet or Sideboard is the new style circular end, with closets in the ends and center part; the back has mirrors in it; the marble is of extra thickness, and of either white Italian, Brocadilla, Tennessee, or black and gold; white looks best on walnut, and Brocadilla or Tennessee on oak; the carving is merely sufficient to carry out the design; the rest is relieved with bold and effective mouldings; the size is five feet four inches long by two feet wide.

The Dining-table is of the center-table pattern, that is, with pillars and plinth; it is either four feet, four feet six inches, or five feet wide, and twelve, fourteen, or sixteen feet long, according to the width. The general character of the table corresponds with the sideboard.

The Service Table, as shown, has three shelves, but by touching a spring the top leaf lowers and the under one rises to meet the center leaf, when it is not all in use; it is a very convenient article for side-dishes and dessert.

The Chair is either cane-seat and back, or stuffed, without springs, in any material required; the pattern can be varied to suit a purchaser.

Fig. 1. *Fig. 2.*

GODEY'S LADY'S BOOK, 1849

Fig. 1 is a very plain style of curtains, hanging on a round pole supported at each end by a bracket, of which *f* is a section. The rings running on the pole are of brass or iron, gilt or bronzed.

Fig. 2 is a cottage window curtain in the Grecian style. The bracket, of which *r* is a sectional view, is of brass, screwed to a lath.

Curtains For Country Houses

Curtains.—Large double windows, or those that open lengthwise like a door, are difficult to fit with lambrequins and curtains; but a light wire or cane frame projecting from over the window, deep enough to permit the blinds and windows to swing clear, can be fastened above the window, and both lambrequin and curtain suspended from that with very good effect. There is nothing more refreshing than plain white Swiss muslin curtains, open in the middle, looped back on either side with a broad band of insertion, over blue, green, or cherry ribbon. Or a strip of well-glazed paper muslin looks as well as ribbon, is much less expensive, and can be purchased in almost all of the delicate colors. Or the curtain may be simply tied back with ribbon. There should be a broad hem on each curtain, with ribbon or paper muslin laid inside the hem. By joining the hem to the curtain with a handsome insertion, and sewing a ruffle on the outer edge of the broad hem neatly fluted, one secures a charming effect from the parlor curtains. Lace curtains are very elegant, but difficult to do up so as to look like new, and somewhat expensive if one hire them cleaned by a French cleaner; and are no more beautiful than these Swiss curtains, which can be easily cleaned, and fluted, and look new each time.

Lambrequins, made also of white Swiss to match the curtains, produce a very airy, cheerful effect, or the lambrequins can be made of damask, or cretonne, with its rich, soft colors, and trimmed with heavy fringe. If one has not confidence in one's own skill to cut and shape these lambrequins, any upholsterer will shape them, and then it is easy work to trim and put them up.

Mrs. H. Beecher, ALL AROUND THE HOUSE, 1879

Noteworthy Suggestions

Having introduced to the reader the specific plans, etc., which will guide him in the erection of a home, a few general words of advice and suggestion will be in order.

It will be well to remember that no architect allows himself, when planning a house, to be guided by any cast-iron set of rules.

A house is a good deal like a suit of clothes, of which a fair fit may be obtained at the ready-made store, while, if close-fitting and stylish garments are wanted, the man's measure is taken and the articles made to order. In the country care should be taken not to make the house too high. Ground is cheap, and a home in the country which spreads over a goodly extent of ground has a certain air of elbow-room and capacity about it that the most magnificent four-story city dwelling fails to possess.

When building projections, window sills, etc., take care to provide a "deep molding" underneath, so that rain-water will drip off. Otherwise it will gather up the dust upon them and run down the walls, leaving mouldy streaks behind.

Where there is no plumbing in the house, the best place for the bath-room is next to the kitchen. Have the range placed against the bath-room partition and place a large tin boiler on the back of the range. From the back of the boiler carry a faucet through the partition to open over a bath-tub. By this means the carrying of water to and fro is dispensed with. To discharge the water from the bath, run a small pipe to a distance of twenty feet from the house and let it end there in a large hole filled in with loose stones and covered with earth. The water when discharged into this hole will soak away into the ground and do no harm, as it is not polluted.

To avoid rats or fire spreading through a house it is advisable to put one course of bricks in mortar at each floor level in all the furrings and partitions.

For the finest effect of foliage use trees and shrubbery as a background and flanking for the principal building. Too many large trees in the foreground cut off the view; besides, they keep out the sunshine, prevent free atmospheric circulation, and injure the house by concentrating upon it dampness and shade.

When a low site for a dwelling cannot be avoided be careful to have a thorough system of under-draining. See that the cellar-wall is raised considerably above the ground and that enough soil is spread around the house to make a yard which will shed the water readily. In a case of this kind every sanitary advantage offered by sun, soil, shelter and prospect should be carefully improved.

A square house includes more space within a given length of wall than any rectangular shape.

Of the whole house the front, and of the front the main entrance, should show the most pains in the direction of ornamentation.

Care in the disposition of rooms will save thousands of steps to those who do the house-work. Kitchen and dining-room should always be adjoining apartments. The dining-room is the place for the china closet. A wood-shed connecting with the kitchen by a covered way is a great convenience in inclement weather.

A multiplicity of closets is an invaluable boon to the housewife.

Frame houses exclude the cold much better if the studding is covered with tongued and grooved sheathing, and this in turn by tarred paper, the weather-boarding being placed over the whole. The sheathing and weather-boarding should be fitted closely around door and window frames, and the tarred paper allowed to lap over a little where a crack is likely to occur.

Where ingrain carpets, usually a yard wide, are to be used, the economical cutting will be helped by having either the length or breadth of each room some multiple of the width, as fifteen feet, eighteen feet, etc.

The difference between slate-roofing and shingles is about two cents per square foot, and where the former is used the difference in outlay purchases practically everlasting durability, a fire-proof roof, and purer rain-water in the cistern.

If free from sap, shingles will last from twenty to thirty years.

An attic, running the full length of the house, with windows at both ends, will prove a fine drying-room in bad weather.

PEALE'S POPULAR EDUCATOR, 1883

SELECTED READING

◆ ◆ ◆

Berg, Donald J., Ed. *Homestead Hints: A Compendium of Useful Information From the Past for the Home, Garden, and Household.* Berkeley, Cal.: Ten Speed Press, 1986.

_____ , Ed. *How to Build in the Country: Good Advice from the Past on How to Choose a Site, Plan, Design, Build, Landscape & Furnish Your Home in the Country.* Berkeley, Cal.: Ten Speed Press, 1986.

Cleveland, Henry W., William Backus and Samuel D. Backus, *Village & Farm Cottages.* 1856. Reprint. Watkins Glen, N.Y.: American Life Foundation, 1982.

Downing, A. J.: *The Architecture of Country Houses.* 1850. Reprint. Mineola, N.Y.: Dover Publications, 1969.

_____ *Victorian Cottage Residences.* 1873. Reprint. Mineola, N.Y.: Dover Publications, 1981.

Grow, Lawrence. *Classic Old House Plans: Three Centuries of American Domestic Architecture.* Pittstown, N. J.: The Main Street Press, 1984.

_____ *Country Architecture: Old-Fashioned Designs for Gazebos, Summerhouses, Springhouses, Smokehouses, Stables, Greenhouses, Carriage Houses, Outhouses, Icehouses, Barns, Doghouses, Sheds, and Other Outbuildings.* Pittstown, N.J.: The Main Street Press, 1985.

_____ *More Classic Old House Plans: Authentic Designs for Colonial and Victorian Homes.* Pittstown, N.J.: The Main Street Press, 1986.

Lawrence, Martin. *The Country Gardener's Almanac.* Pittstown, N.J.: The Main Street Press, 1984.

Vaux, Calvert. *Villas & Cottages.* 1857. Reprint. Mineola, N.Y.: Dover Publications, 1970.

Weidenmann, Jacob. *Beautifying Country Homes.* 1870. Reprint. Watkins Glen, N.Y.: American Life Foundation, 1982.

Index

◆ ◆ ◆

Donald Berg, an architect, lives and works in Rockville Centre, New York. His column, HOMESTEAD HINTS, appears in newspapers across the country.